HIMADRI HOUSING SOCIETY

HIMADRI HOUSING SOCIETY

ALOK BHATTACHARYA

Worldwide Published by
Pendown Press

PENDOWN PRESS

An ISO 9001 & ISO 14001 Certified Co.,
Regd. Office: 2525/193, 1st Floor, Onkar Nagar-A,
Tri Nagar, Delhi-110035
Ph.: 09350849407, 09312235086
E-mail: info@pendownpress.com
Branch Office: 1A/2A, 20, Hari Sadan, Ansari Road,
Daryaganj, New Delhi-110002
Ph.: 011-45794768
Website: PendownPress.com

First Edition: 2019

ISBN: 978-93-89601-23-7

Layout and Cover Designed by Pendown Graphics Team
Printed and Bound in India by Thomson Press India Ltd.

CONTENTS

PREFACE

Four or f ve decades into the post-independent India, a newly aff uent middle class is emerging up in the urban centers who live in the f ats of multi-storey buildings, having come there in search of a better life. These people have left behind their individual geographical identities, to form a new culture.

These people have discovered the new secret mantra for being competitive and successful in the 20th-century industrial society and that is "economics is the most important driving force to carry forward the aspirations of the society, all other considerations being secondary."

Modern India is becoming more and more materialistically oriented and so is increasing the growing inf uence of money power in achieving your goals or also in bending the rules of the establishment. The hard-working middle-class parents are providing a comfortable life and good access to higher education to their children, who in their turn are pursuing better and new careers. In pursuit of a better life, they often land in the greener pastures of the developed countries and settle down there. This is an emerging trend in Urban India.

This new trend is, however, creating new problems for the parents, who cannot anymore bank upon the availability and support of the children during their advancing old age. Thus they have to look for outside support to lead their retired life independently, some move to the 'Old Age Homes' towards the end of their lives.

The book is the story of the urban middle class. Hope the readers will f nd it interesting.

—Alok Bhattacharya

About the Author

After his Ph.D. in Chemistry from BHU, the author went for further studies in Canada and joined CSIR as a scientist on return. Moving on to industry, he retired as General Manager (R&D) after a successful career. He is a very widely travelled person and post-retirement has taken to writing as a hobby, on wide-ranging subjects. He has published Six books–Global warming, 2008 (Rupa & Co.); India: The oldest surviving civilization 2010 (B.R. Publishing Corp.), two novels–Dreams are worth chasing, 2010; Love is where your heart is, 2011 (both by diamond Books), Mankind: Origin, Journey to the Present and Future, 2018, When Travel Bug Bites Sam, 2018, (both by GPH Books). This is his seventh publication. He can be contacted at his e-mail address: dralokb@yahoo.co.in.

About the Book

The housing society inhabitants represent a cross-section of contemporary urban culture. Arora is a rich building contractor having great faith in the power of money. Manish, a college student suffers from a guilt complex, because of his having a different sexual orientation and feels comfortable, for the f rst time in his life, after he moves over to USA and becomes a part of the 'gay' community of New York. Kamlesh, a Delhi University student lands in USA after she is hurriedly married to a suave NRI and to her horror discovers that he is already married to an American girl and who ultimately deserts her. Abandoned and lost in a new country, she struggles alone for f ve long years to bounce back into the mainstream and then meets a brilliant neurosurgeon from Kanpur.

Mrs. Gulati, after becoming a widow, learns to lead an independent life without becoming a burden on anybody while Agrawal, a lonely senior citizen, after the death of his wife from cancer, struggles with the problems of old age and decides to live and die at his own terms. There are many more interesting characters interwoven in the plot and gives the story a wider dimension.

-1-

The laughter club on that particular morning was operating in full swing in the usual corner of a South Delhi park. It was just around sunrise time and the joggers and morning walk addicts were returning from their daily quota of well-spent time. The laughter club members had gathered in a large circle of around thirty members, mostly in their middle or advanced ages, were practising the rituals of clapping, followed by bursting into a guffaw, the boisterous laughter originating from their inner bellies, along with the full movement of their upper body parts. The echo of the full blast of the combined laughter was reverberating throughout the park and beyond, forcing the passersby to turn and look into the source and move on with a smile. After f ve more minutes of this heavy exercise, the group dispersed for the day and broke into small sub-groups. All the members knew each other well.

It happened to be a Saturday so nobody was in a hurry to go back. In fact, the Saturday was especially attractive as the members played host in rotation, to serve tea/coffee snacks to the entire group. Tea and snacks were already placed neatly on a bench, bought by the servant of Kanwal Kishore Arora, who happened to be the President of the club for the year, that day being his turn. Arora was a rich contractor engaged in building houses and off ces, of around f fty years of age, residing in a duplex f at of the Neelachal Apartments. He invited everybody to help themselves and the bonhomie and small talks abounded along with the breakfast. Arora was talking to Santanu Chakravarty "Kamlesh has asked me to remind you to tell Bipasha to come to her at nine A.M sharp."

Santanu nodded "O.K."

Santanu Chakravarty, around forty-f ve, was an engineer working in Engineers India Ltd. (E.I.L) at Bhikaji Cama Place, residing in the adjacent Himadri Apartments. His daughter Bipasha and Kamlesh were class fellows in Lady Irwin School and were good friends. Pahuja called Agarwal who was considered an expert in stock market affairs from the other side and asked "Agarwalji, I was looking for you regarding some investment in Apollo Tyres and Tata Steels. How do you feel about their convertible debentures? Agrawal replied, "sounds O.K. Though I feel Tata Steel is f nancially a much more stable company".

Joginder Singh Pahuja, a burly Sikh of around 48 years was residing in Manas Apartments, working in Central Warehousing Corporation (CWC) and lived very lavishly f aunting his money power, he regularly dabbled in the stock market. Laxmi Narain Agrawal had just retired from Larsen & Toubro, was residing in Himadri Apartment and was believed to have made good money in share market. Before the members dispersed, it was decided that next Saturday's breakfast would be hosted by Retd. Brigadier Brar from nearby S-Block of G.K.-II. Agarwal and Santanu came together to Himadri Apartment where both of them resided.

Santanu was a Bengali hailing from Midnapur and had done his engineering from Jadavpur University. He was in the EIL for the last twelve years, had joined the company in Duliajan, Assam and was presently in the design cell of their Petrochemical Division. He had recently come back from a two-year deputation stint in Iran. During his Iran posting his family stayed in Himadri Apartment where he had also been allotted a f at through the lucky draw of Delhi Development Authority (DDA). His wife Indrani was from Kolkata and was teaching in Rajagiri Public School, just across the road. It was a missionary school managed by a Kerala Christian Diocese and was considered a good school of the city. Her son Parthasarthy was a student in the same school in class eight and his sister Bipasha was studying in class ten in lady Irwin School. Bipasha and Kamlesh were class fellows and on every Saturday and Sunday, they used to do joint study, alternatively in each other's house. Today she had to go to Kamlesh to the Neelachal Apartments just across the road.

Laxmi Narain Agarwal had recently retired from L & T from the post of Finance Manager and was quite computer savvy. He had a computer in his house which was quite rare in those days. He had a three-bedroom ground f oor f at in Himadri Apartment. His wife

Nandini was teaching classical vocal music (Bhatkhande School) at her home and had six or seven students, Bipasha and Kamlesh also among them and being in the second year of the class. Agarwals had three daughters, all married, one in Ludhiana, other at Ambala and the youngest at Dehradun. He was currently the President of the Resident Welfare Association (RWA) of Himadri Apartment with Santanu as the Security-in-charge of the Managing Committee (M.C.).

-2-

A very nasty incident had occurred last night at Himadri Apartment and an emergency meeting of the M.C. had been called, in the RWA off ce, by the President. Agarwal asked Santanu to brief the Committee about the facts. Santanu started "as all of you know, both the gates of the apartment are closed by the President's order, after eleven P.M. for security reasons and are to be opened thereafter, on making entry in the RWA register, of the f at number and vehicle number of the entrant along with the resident's signature. Visitors are not allowed to park their vehicles inside, after eleven P.M. unless their names and the resident's f at number is entered in the RWA register" he looked around and everybody nodded.

He continued "In f at No. 278, lives a spinster of around 35 years named Miss Sudeshna Singh. She is a tenant and lives alone working in some private f rm".

Members were now curious. Kaul, who was the Vice-President asked: "that smart lady with boy-cut hair, always wearing jeans and western dresses?"

Bajaj – the secretary quipped "hey Kaul! Does bhabhiji know that you are observing her so closely?

Subramanium – the treasurer added, "my wife tells me that Miss Singh is not very much liked by ladies and she also avoids the company of ladies."

Santanu continued "Anyway, coming back to the point, it so happens she has several smart-looking young male visitors who generally come around ten o'clock at night and leave only after midnight."

Singhal–a member of MC commented "Interesting! very interesting!! I wonder what do they do at such late hours?" Kaul shrugged "Any body's guess?" Santanu protested "what goes on inside the f at is none of our business but what happened after the guest came out last night after midnight is the point we have assembled here to discuss"

Everybody became alert "what happened?"

"The guest asked the guard to open the gate to let the car go out" he looked at the members.

Singhal asked, "and then?"

"the guard on night duty asked him to sign in the RWA register and f ll the details i.e. the f at number, name and the vehicle number. The visitor refused, a big haughty argument followed and the other guard from Gate No. 2 also joined. The guest threatened the guard and unable to have his way ultimately called the lady, who came and right away charged the guard menacingly that how he could dare to insult her guest?" he looked at Singhal who asked, "and then?"

"The guard insisted the lady to sign the register and showed her the President's order. At this, the lady slapped the guard hard on his cheek but still refused to sign the register. By this time, hearing the commotion another guard on patrolling duty at the rear, also came and on f nding the situation going out of control, came running to my f at, woke me from sleep and I reached the spot. It was around two at night.

Kaul nodded in disbelief "that lady is very aggressive but you can't hit a guard?"

Santanu continued "Anyway, I tried to calm her down by reasoning that the guard was only performing his duty and it was for the safety of the residents themselves but the lady did not calm down and started shouting at me," he looked around, then started "I countered by telling her that slapping a guard on duty is an offence in the eyes of law and told the visitor to sign the register so that the guard could open the gate and that we would sort out the matter with Miss Singh in the morning." Subramanium asked, "Did the visitor sign?" "Yes, he complied, the gate was opened and he went away but the lady was bent on creating a scene and was still shouting at me."

Singhal got agitated "you also should have slapped her right there"

"In fact, I would have very much liked to do just that as she was getting on my nerves and also I was getting irritated but good sense somehow prevailed and I left the scene after telling her that we would talk about it, in the morning after she returned to her good senses".

He looked at the President "Now, what would be our line of action especially since all the guards are very agitated and are demanding an apology from the lady?"

After long deliberations, the f nal draft of a letter was prepared by the Secretary and it was agreed that this letter would be sent by the President summoning her to appear before the MC on or before next Sunday evening and apologies for her bad behavior last Friday night slapping the guard on duty, along with a copy of the letter to her landlord residing in Chandni Chowk to warn the lady to follow the rules of RWA or face the consequences. The guard was also asked to give a complaint in writing which some members wanted to be forwarded to the police. Thus a post-script to the letter was added:

In case of non-compliance, the written complaint of the guard against you, along with a copy of this letter, will be sent to the police for necessary action as per law.

Surendra Nath Kaul was a Kashmiri Pandit and a tall handsome man of around forty-f ve or so and was Asst. Manager in the Bank of Baroda, Parliament Street branch. His father was Dy. Secretary in the Ministry of Home Affairs who after retirement had settled in Vasant Vihar, a posh locality of South Delhi. Subramanium worked in the f nance dept. of Central Warehousing Corporation and was a colleague of Pahuja residing in Manas and was a few years younger to him. His name was abbreviated to Subra by which name he was generally called and hailed from Tiruchirapally of Tamilnadu, was a Tambram (Tamil Brahmin), was living in Delhi for last twenty years, was a strict vegetarian and a religious man. Bajaj was from Ambala, had set up a computer peripheral shop in Nehru Place and was almost completely bald though he was only forty or so.

<h1 style="text-align:center">-3-</h1>

Kamlesh was a tall pretty, fair-complexioned girl, her best friend Bipasha had come to her house in Neelachal Apartments and they were having the joint study session, in her room on the upper f oor for more than two hours. Poonam, the mother of Kamlesh, entered the room with tea and pakauris and called for a break from studies. Poonam had a beauty parlour in the Alkapuri market and before leaving for the parlour had come for some chatting with the girls and asked Bipasha"how is Indrani?

Bipasha replied "Aunty, she is very busy, evaluating like mad, the exam papers, as the marks are to be submitted the day after tomorrow. In fact, right after breakfast she almost pushed me and Partho out of the house and asked us not to come back before lunchtime."

Poonam started laughing, Bipasha had a knack of saying things in a humorous way. She said "by the way, please remind Indrani to f nish her engagements as the next sitting of the kitty party would be held in her house.

"I will, aunty your Pakauris are lovely". Poonam turned to Kamlesh "Please keep an eye on the maid working downstairs" and left.

Aroras had a son Harish studying in class eight in St. Columba's is in Gole Market. He had gone to Partho to Play table tennis in his apartment. Arora used to go to his off ce in M block market of G.K.- II a little later and was still in the house doing some off ce work as well as watching a T.V. serial. He had a f ourishing business and was considered a successful man.

Indrani was furiously evaluating the exam papers in order to meet the deadline. One set of answer sheets still remained and she was running short of time so she asked Santanu who was watching

T.V. "Please order lunch from Naba Gita. I have no time for cooking". Santanu ordered four meals. Naba Gita was a free home delivery service restaurant in Chittaranjan Park serving steaming hot Bengali food-both veg. and non-veg. in tiff n careers and had a wide clientele among the Bengalis living in the area.

Downstairs in the spare car garage on the ground f oor, Partho and his friends were playing table tennis and the shouting and the din was audible in the whole block. The garage was lying vacant earlier and was quite big, without any doors, with a side entrance also and was the RWA property. Members of the block, all of whom had school-going children, had jointly decided to make use of the common space, had contributed to buy a table tennis table and net. The garage was f tted with tube lights at both the ends and a contributory table tennis club was started with a fee of Rs. ten per month to meet the recurring expenses. The idea proved to be a great success, so much so, that boys and girls made a beeline to become a member and it remained crowded all the time. Ramesh Chandra Baluja, who lived on the f rst f oor, was made the convener of the club. He had retired from Reserve Bank of India Jaipur last year and had settled here with his wife, had two daughters, both married, one staying in Delhi and the other at Pune.

Among the SFS apartments in Alkapuri, Himadri Apartment was the last one to be occupied and though it had more than four hundred f ats more than one hundred f ats still remained unoccupied. In the block where Baluja and Santanu lived, nine f ats were occupied out of the thirteen. The residents of this block had jointly decided to hold a dinner get together once in a month, turn by turn and tonight it started with Anand as he was the f rst occupant in the block. Anand was the proprietor of a transport company and had his off ce at Desh Bandhu Gupta Road. He had a daughter Anju studying in class seven in Greenf eld School near Tara Apartment and a son Rakesh Studying in Class four in St. Vivekanand School in Lajpat Nagar. His wife was a homemaker. The party was a great success.

ooo

-4-

Joginder Singh Pahuja was a member of the laughter club and lived in Manas Apartments in a very lavish style. Two years back he had purchased a new Fiat car on cash payment. Last year he had sent his son, after graduation, to England for studying M.B.A. and this year his daughter Priyanka, after doing I Sc. with average marks from Modern School, had been admitted for engineering studies in Galgotia Institute at Noida with a hefty capitation fee. His wife Aparna was an interior decorator and had an off ce in Alkapuri market. She had a full-time cook cum maid to assist her in household affairs.

Pahuja often threw drink parties at his residence and this time it was to celebrate his daughter's admission in engineering college. He had invited Santanu and Arora also along with some of his Manas friends. His f at was very tastefully decorated though a bit overstuffed with decorative pieces. He was also a member of the Panchsheel Club in Panchsheel Enclave. Pahuja worked in C.W.C. near the airport and was a very amiable and high spirited host. Mutton tikka, cashew nut and Pakauries were served in plenty with each round of drinks and the host ensured that everybody was fully sozzled before he left.

Santanu often wondered how could Pahuja maintain such a lavish lifestyle being in a lower post than him in a public sector and during some casual discussion with Subramanium who also worked in C.W.C, he mentioned it. Subra was not amused and whispered to him in a conf dential tone. "Pahuja is stores-in-charge and I am in f nance in the same off ce. A lot of bungling has been lately detected by our internal audit dept. among the store inventories. A conf dential internal enquiry is going on against Pahuja. Lots of old stocks have been found unaccounted and have been shown as written off. It is suspected that these materials are being disposed of in the open market but the modus operandi is not known and nothing has been proved as yet. He could be in serious diff culty, if they get some proof."

The Managing Committee members had assembled in the RWA off ce for their monthly meeting. Kaul was looking very gloomy. Agrawal asked him "hey Kaul! you look very depressed, have you again quarrelled with your wife?". Kaul did not cheer up "No, no, this time it is much more serious".

Agrawal was getting impatient "you love to keep going round and round the point, why don't you straightway come to the point, what is it that is troubling you?" Everybody looked at Kaul.

"I have been promoted." Singhal and Bajaj jointly shouted "congrats! let there be a party right away. What a way to break the good news and we thought.......". But Kaul was still not enthused "But there is a rider"

"What?" Subramanium, as if asked on behalf of everybody.

"I have been transferred to Surat in Gujarat" and that seemed to diffuse everybody. He continued "I have to join there within a fortnight and so here is my resignation from the RWA" he delivered the letter to Agrawal.

Santanu enquired "but surely you can get some extension pleading that your son is in High School and his exams start next week?"

"I tried that but Head off ce says that Surat branch is without a Branch Manager for more than the last three months and now the No.2 man, Parekh is proceeding on leave by end of this month for his daughter's marriage. His leave has already been sanctioned."

Bajaj asked, "could you not decline the promotion?"

Kaul negatived the suggestion "I had already declined a promotion three years back and so for the last eight years I am on the same post, whereas my juniors have got promotions and moved ahead".

Santanu asked, "what does bhabhi ji say?"

"Sukriti is very f rm that I should not decline the promotion this time as it would be bad for my career. She says she will manage things at this end".

Sukriti was a school teacher in the Army Public School on the Ridge Road near Dhaula Kuan. Kauls had purchased a Maruti car last year and she was learning driving to be able to drive to the school. Their daughter Shweta was already studying in class seven there and she was planning to get their son Ritwick also admitted in class eleven next session in her school so that all three could commute to the school by the car together. Sukriti felt that with Ritwick's help she will manage to get the outdoor jobs done. Thus Pasricha was inducted as vice president of the RWA, Kaul was given a send-off by the RWA and he left within a fortnight.

The Kitty Party for the month was held at Indrani's house. The ladies Kitty Party had twenty members, mostly middle-aged ladies, majority of them housewives and on the f abby side. The party was held on a monthly basis in each member's house and decided by lottery. The host was presented a kitty of twenty thousand rupees, against a contribution of ₹1000/- per month. The party started at four on Thursday and ended by six in the evening before the husbands came back from the off ce, thus it did not suit the off ce going ladies, consequently, housewives, school teachers and self-employed ladies were the members. The host used to give a prize for punctuality for the earliest arrival, to be decided by lottery if more than one claimant was eligible, to induce members to come in time. In return, the other members gave a surprise gift collectively, to the host apart from the kitty money.

Generally the ladies were in good terms with each other, some had tendency to show off, but some of them had abrasive relations like Mrs.Parikh could not stand Mrs. Oberoi and Mrs. Pahuja had a great rivalry with Mrs. Srivastava whose husband was top-notch in some private company and was hardly in talking terms with her though both were staying in the same block in Manas Apartment. Indrani, as a host, took care that such people should not be seated side by side. Mrs. Srivastava and Poonam were the f rst to arrive with the former in her chauffeur-driven Ambassador car, though Manas was hardly 200 yards away. They were followed by Sukriti and Mrs. Subramanium. Within ten minutes the house was full and cold drinks were circulated.

Mrs. Pahuja announced, "we are planning to go to England this summer to meet our son". Mrs. Oberoi casually informed, "we are planning a week's holiday in Kashmir during May." Mrs. Parkih pointed towards a cute diamond locket worn by Mrs. Srivastava in her necklace who promptly unchained it and showed it around telling that her husband, during his Europe tour last month, had bought it from Amsterdam. Mrs. Pahuja showed no interest in the diamond and went on talking to Mrs. Pandey of Neelachal Apartments. Time for a game of housie had come. Poonam conducted the game and Mrs. Pandey won the full house amounting to ₹200/-

It was time for snacks and tea. Hot caulif ower Pakauras were served by Bipasha who was helping her mother, followed by green pea ghugni which had to be repeated due to heavy demand. Next came sandwiches and lastly came a Bengali sweet-Labang lata prepared by Indrani. Everybody liked it and asked for more. Mrs. Pandey and Poonam asked for the recipe and decided to try it in their homes. The maidservant by now was clearing the dishes and tea was served next. Lottery for the punctuality prize was drawn and went to Poonam and Indrani gave her the prize a set of six glasses. Mrs. Pandey then presented the surprise gift on behalf of everybody to Indrani- a double bed cover along with the Kitty of ₹20,000. The lottery for the next party was drawn and Mrs. Pandey was declared to be next host. The party dispersed by quarter to six.

-5-

Summer had come. Bipasha and Kamlesh had appeared for their high school exams. Priyanka's f rst-year engineering exams were going on. Pahuja was not seen lately in the laughter club and Santanu enquired Subramanium, who is a conf dential tone said: "you remember what I had told you last time regarding the audit enquiry against him?"

Santanu nodded "yes I do, what happened of it?"

Well! The audit found some grave irregularities going on since the last several years in the stores and asked for an explanation from Pahuja, which were, however, not found satisfactory. The vigilance committee, therefore, decided to immediately remove him from the present post and transfer him to Bhopal, a much smaller off ce, consequently he left about a fortnight back to join at Bhopal.

Pasricha the new Vice President of the RWA was a very jovial man, had a huge pot belly and seemed to love it. He was the owner of a big crockery store in G.K. I 'M' Block market, his daughter was married and lived in USA. He had two sons Manish and Anupam, the elder studying in B.Com Final from Dayal Singh college at Lodhi Road and the younger in class twelve from Sardar Patel school. Manish was a very handsome young man though somewhat effeminate type, fair-complexioned and tall. His father had bought him a new motorcycle for commuting to the college. Lately, Manish was often seen with Priyanka, the beautiful daughter of Pahuja. Both made a lovely pair and often played table tennis or were seen strolling together hand in hand in Himadri Apartment or in Alkapuri market or in the Park during evening hours. Priyanka was a mod girl with bobbed hair, wore shorts and top, showing her beautiful legs or in miniskirt and sleeveless blouse. She knew she was beautiful and had an attitude, maintaining an air of hard to approach. Since Pasricha used to come late from his shop and Pahuja were also out of Delhi, the pair used to roam around quite freely. Over a period of time, people got accustomed to seeing them together though the ladies used to feel that this must have been going on with encouragement from Mrs. Pahuja as Manish was a very eligible boy.

There was a vacant big room about 25' X 20' in size, almost the size of a hall, f tted with collapsible gate, lying at the rear side of the eastern end of the apartment, used as a junkyard of the RWA. Pasricha suggested that the room could be used for much better purposes. After much deliberations, the managing committee felt that it could be used as a co-operative grocery shop. The idea evoked a huge general interest from the residents and Pasricha was made in-charge of the project. Members were asked to buy a ₹one hundred share for the stores and over a period of one month forty thousand was collected. The junkyard was cleaned, whitewashed and a committee of three members was constituted to give the project a shape. Pasricha prepared a design in consultation with his committee which needed a lot of woodwork and some renovations in the civil structure as well, costing a lot of money. A further loan of ₹one thousand per member was raised, re-payable after six months of the start of the stores, to be adjusted in terms of grocery items purchased from there, a further sum of ₹forty thousand was collected and the work started, the progress to be watched by residents on day to day basis.

In three months time, the stores became operational. Press wallah's f fteen-year-old son Umesh was employed as a part-time employee of the co-operative stores and the stores were stuffed with provisions bought from the wholesale market of Khari Baoli. It was opened by the President of RWA with much fanfare, Pasricha donated one table and two chairs and some resident donating the old cycle of his son who had grown up now. The cycle was given to Umesh for running the errands and giving home delivery of the monthly grocery to the doorsteps of residents. The committee members and some retired persons volunteered their services. Initially, the stores were kept open from six to nine in the evening with a provision to expand the timing as the business grew.

The stores became a big hit with the housewives who f ocked the stores in the evening. The prices were competitive and many residents switched over to buy the monthly grocery from the stores. All you had to do was to give list if you did not have the time to wait and the provisions were home delivered to you the next morning along with the cash memo whereby you made the cash payment to Umesh. Soon the stores became a meeting place for the ladies and other retired people who would sit in a group in front of the stores and gossip. People were very thankful to Pasricha for implementing this facility.

Bipasha and Kamlesh had both passed their high school with over seventy-f ve per cent marks and opted for the Science stream. Ritwick also did well and was admitted to the Army Public School. Sukriti had learnt driving and was now using the car to commute to the school along with the children. Kaul had come home on a week's leave after six months and encouraged his son to learn the driving so as to be able to help his mother. Partha was a good student, now in class nine in the Rajagiri Public School, Indrani was very strict about his studies and wanted him to study engineering. Harish was in class ten but he was not a good student so Arora had arranged to engage a home tutor who used to give tuitions for Science and Maths. Manish was now doing his MBA from Modinagar, about forty km away from Delhi, en route to Meerut and used to daily commute there on his motorbike.

-6-

Pasricha had heard about the affair of his son with some girl from Manas apartment and one night, after reaching home from his shop, he called Manish to his room and had a closed-door frank talk with him "I understand that you are often seen with a girl, who is she?"

"She is Priyanka Pahuja from Manas apartment, studying engineering"

"Hmmm! How serious is your relationship?"

Manish was not prepared for this "No, dad, it is not serious."

"But people are noticing it"

Manish kept silent. Pasricha continued "My son, now you are grown up, let us have a man to the man talk and listen to me f rst" he looked at Manish "see, you are in your f nal year of MBA. I would feel that you will f rst build up your career. Your sister is in USA and you perhaps don't know what I want you to leave for USA after your MBA to seek a better future, your sister has agreed to sponsor you after you clear your MBA and your jijaji is trying to line up a job for you in his f rm." Manish was pleasantly surprised. This was great news for him and he said "I did not know anything about it?" and looked at his dad.

"Well! You know about it now, I feel this is an opportunity very few lucky people would get and you would be a fool to squander this chance"

Manish immediately replied, "I assure you, dad, I would grab this opportunity at the f rst chance when it comes."

"That is just like my son and so I would advise you not to get involved with girls at this stage, you will get ample chances for that after you give a good shape to your career."

"Thank you, dad, I would def nitely keep it in mind."

Pasricha cautioned him "but don't tell anybody yet about your plans, I repeat anybody, at this stage. When the time comes and if everything goes well, people would come to know about it when it materializes. For the time being you just concentrate to f nish your MBA."

"Thank you, dad, for thinking about my future and I assure you I will clear the MBA in time". Pasricha was satisf ed with his son's attitude, Manish was more than satisf ed with his dream for a bright future.

The table tennis table had been taken over by college going boys from other blocks, who often used to bring their friends from other apartments. They kept playing till late and never vacated the table and so the children of the block, for whom the table had been primarily purchased, did not get any chance at all to play. Moreover, the big boys made so much noise that the residents of the block felt very disturbed. The children of the block, majority of whom were girls, ultimately complained to Baluja in a group "uncle, we never get any chance to play. The big boys from another block most of whom are friends of Manish Bhaiya, don't allow us to play. Please ask them to vacate our table."

Baluja was an upright and a no-nonsense man. He called a meeting of the residents of the block and he, Santanu and Sarin went as a team, next evening, to confront the boys in the middle of an ongoing game. Baluja had an additional point of irritants also. His Fiat car was parked right in front of the garage, hardly f fteen feet away. As there were no place to sit in the area, the onlookers as well as the players in wait, used to sit on the car, three or four on the bonnet, two or three on the mudguards, bumpers and sometimes even on the roof, in all about ten to twelve boys, cheering the players in full blasts. Baluja had several times asked the boys to get down from the car but to no avail. The moment he disappeared, the boys would climb back to continue the fun and frolic.

Baluja barged in, caught the ball in the mid-air and straight away came to the point "We had purchased this table primarily for the children of our block and they complain that you don't allow them to play?" The boy who was on the other side of the table vehemently protested "No uncle, we have never said so."

"But you don't vacate the table, which implies the same thing". The other boy argued, "we have also paid to be the members, so we also have the right to play".

Sarin was annoyed by such audacity and countered "we had purchased the table for the children of our block." Manish chipped in "but the garage is a common space, meant for everybody" Santanu pointed out "look, you also have a similar empty garage in your block and nobody prevents you from buying your own table."

One of the boys asked "Uncle, are you asking us not to play here any more?"

Baluja intervened "No doubt, we would be very happy if you could become so considerate but besides that, there are certainly other issues as well."

The boys in unison asked "what?"

One is that some of you are not only non-members of this Club, but are not even the residents of this apartment and Baluja pointed out to both the players who were playing.

Another boy from Himadri apartment whose friends were playing protested "in sports such restrictions would not allow the players to grow."

Sarin quipped "very lofty ideal! Then why don't you open a club in Manas apartment and open it up for the whole of Delhi?" he pointed out to the boys, both of whom were from Manas.

The boys were cornered and so now getting agitated. Sensing that Baluja, in a tone of compromise, said "look here boys, we are not against your playing here, but with so many people around, it becomes quite crowded with the effect that nobody gets enough time to play. Moreover, if you keep playing up to at nine o'clock you won't be able to study and your parents would blame us for allowing you to play till so late."

Manish vehemently protested "No, uncle, no"

Baluja continued "also remember that the crowd, shouting and the general din you create, disturbs the other residents of the block and so some time limit has to be maintained as well.

The boys asked in unison "and what would be that?"

Baluja in an authoritative tone said "seven P.M. only, as the exams are coming". The boys said, "uncle, make it seven-thirty."

Baluja looked at Sarin and Santanu, who said: "provided the lights of the garage are punctually switched off at seven-thirty."

Baluja concluded, "let it be implemented from today itself as it is already past seven-thirty and he switched off the lights. Reluctantly the boys left.

Next morning, while going for the morning walk, Santanu noticed that every inch of Baluja's car was plastered with posters from the Delhi University's ongoing election campaign stickers including the windscreen, side view mirror, window glasses, rear glass, bonnet, doors and the whole body including the bumpers as well.

However, this altercation with boys had some statutory effect. The number of boys was reduced and noise levels also came down. Manish organized cleaning of the garage in the other block and in two months time, another T.T. club became operational in the other block, to the relief of the children of this block.

-7-

Priyanka and Manish continued to be often seen together even in the new T.T. Club where she was a regular visitor. Priyanka was a mod girl, had been a student of Modern School and was no stranger to the ways of boys. She knew how to keep them on a leash, her formula was to give them only one-quarter of what they wanted and that way she retained her control over her admirers. However, she was quite puzzled with the behaviour of Manish who never seemed to madly need her body, even though she was quite willing to yield to him if only he demanded it. He seemed quite different, may be having extraordinary self-control over his male hormonal urges. They were good friends, were going out together for more than may be two years and also were alone in each other's company, so many times but he had never made any sexual advances, always maintained a decent friendly limit and she never felt threatened with his masculinity.

Once when Aparna had gone to Bhopal to her husband for a few days, Priyanka had invited Manish to her house. She was going to take her bath when he came in. They were completely alone, she asked him to sit in the drawing-room and went to take her bath. She was feeling very much sexually aroused and after the bath came out wrapped only in her towels, went and clung to him with urgent urge to go all the way. he embraced her, kissed her, fondled her breasts and in the process her towel fell on the f oor and she stood completely naked in his arms. He saw her private parts, touched it and even admired her beautiful body but was not somehow burning with desire, retained his self-control, did not press for more and more and after some time they got disengaged. Her femininity had been deeply wounded, she felt that it must have been her fault somehow that she could not arouse him. She could not pinpoint what exactly was lacking but had a hunch that some spark was missing in him. May be he was too frigid or culturally very much inhibited about casual sex, or having traditional sexual morality angle or may be impotent. Whatever it was, she was unable to seduce him.

They remained good friends though, kept going out together after that also, continued to remain good friends and externally maintained the facade of being very intimate with each other. All the girls of the neighbourhood were very much envious of her and to everybody's knowledge Manish was her boyfriend but internally she started feeling dissatisf ed with the relationship, but there was a positive side to her relationship with Manish. The boys of the locality had accepted her relationship with him, as a result, she felt secure in their company and from their advances to her. It could thus be said that Manish the man, had provided her with the security especially as her brother and father were away, even though he could not provide her with the intimate biological satisfaction. Her mother also was in agreement with this angle and was not unduly worried about the safety of her grown-up daughter within the locality, a big relief to the mother.

Manish was very disturbed the day he came back from the house of Priyanka. He was upset because he could not put the f nal seal in consummating the man-woman, relationship. She was a beautiful girl, had lovely f gures and also had fully yielded to him, eager to be consumed. But strangely he did not feel any urge, even though she would be the fantasy of any young man and yet he disappointed her. Why did his hormone chemistry not respond to her invitation? What was wrong with him? Was he impotent? This line of self-analysis ultimately led to the darkest of his secrets which he wanted to keep locked in the innermost chamber of mind for fear of strong disapproval from the society and relatives.

When Manish was, may be in class f ve or six in the school, his family used to go to vacations to their native village Nakodar near Jalandhar in Punjab. They used to play in the sugarcane and wheat f elds during the winter months. The elder brother of his fast friend Surinder was very friendly to him. Once while wandering through the f elds in the afternoon alone, he bumped into the elder brother who at that time was working alone in his wheat f eld, uprooting the weeds. They started talking and while walking together he led Manish to the sugarcane f eld. Once deep inside the bushes, he caught hold of him and before Manish could even protest, got him undressed, made him lie down and sodomised him. Next year when they went to their village again, Surinder told him that his elder brother was selected in the army and had gone away.

When Manish was in class eleven, he went to Ranikhet during summer for an NCC Camp, for a fortnight. Their instructor, a thickset muscular young man took a fancy for him and on a Sunday took him to Chakrata for showing the apple orchards. While there, in a remote place, the instructor sodomised him, the worst thing is that he liked it. The instructor paid him also for keeping it a secret and repeated the act next week also when all other boys had gone for sightseeing. On reopening of the school after Summer vacations, Manish learnt that the instructor had been dismissed from the service for his immoral activities.

Manish was now in the f nal year of his MBA at Modinagar. Last year he got friendly with a f nal year student, Bhupinder Singh Tikait– a tall athletic Jat, who took a fancy for him. When Tikait used to look into his eyes, some sort a vibration started in his body. They got closer or could be said that they got attracted to each other and once Tikait took him to his hostel on the pretext of giving some useful notes and once in his room he sodomised him. Manish did not even like to admit to himself but seemed to enjoy the act. He was shocked when he heard next month that Tikait had been expelled from the college for attempting to sodomise fellow hostellers.

Manish felt upset today because he felt he was different from other men and had a deep sense of guilt for having a different sexual orientation for an unnatural act. The man-woman relationship was natural and considered necessary for the preservation of the species and was thus an agreeable norm whereas the society had a great contempt for a man to man sexual relationship. Thus he had to hide his feelings from everybody around him and this created a sense of guilt. He was ready to give anything to be like other young men but it seemed his own nature wanted it otherwise. Why had he been made different? Was it a temporary or a permanent aberration?

-8-

It was around ten in the morning. Santanu had just f nished the departmental meeting and going out to meet a client in Nehru Place when the telephone bell rang. It was from his wife Indrani and she was speaking from the school with a great sense of urgency. She asked him to come home immediately and informed "I was in a class when I was called at the Principal's off ce for an urgent call from Mrs. Baluja. She was panicky and with a trembling voice informed that as usual Mr. Baluja had gone to toilet but it was more than one hour and he was still not coming out. The bathroom door was bolted from inside and in spite of her frantic calls and knocking at the door there was no response from inside. All her attempts to break open the door had failed and so in desperation, she had called just now. I am going home immediately and if the worst has happened I won't be able to handle the situation alone. So please come immediately." She put down the receiver.

Santanu rushed out after rescheduling his meeting. On reaching home he found several ladies in Mrs. Baluja's f at, but all the men had gone to the off ce and no action had been taken. Mrs. Baluja was crying uncontrollably and ladies including Indrani were consoling her. On seeing her husband Indrani asked, "Do something immediately to break open the door."

Santanu tried his best but in spite of his repeated pushes and proddings, the door did not budge. He next called two security guards from the gate and their joint effort was successful in breaking open the door f nally. What they saw was a very heart-rending scene. Baluja was sitting on his toilet seat with his pyjama down and in a reclined position with the cistern, his eyes wide open but expressionless. Santanu shoved him a bit and asked his well being but this act imbalanced him and the body, which had become cold, fell down sideways. It was quite obvious that he was dead. Mrs. Baluja who had silently crept in from behind and was peeping, uttered an agonizing piercing cry and fainted. Some other ladies immediately caught hold of her and escorted her to the bedroom to lie down.

In the meantime, Santanu straightened the body, tied the cords of the pyjama and with the help of the guards took the body out of the bathroom and laid it on a bedcover spread on the f oor of the dining room after setting the dining table and chairs aside. Having laid the body, he asked Indrani to inform his daughters immediately. Mrs. Baluja had not yet come to her senses, so Indrani searched the telephone book lying on the table and f rst phoned her daughter Garima living in Sarojini Nagar telling her what had happened and asking her to come immediately. Garima phoned her sister in Pune and then started. Santanu went to fetch a doctor and asked the guards to stay there. The doctor examined the body, said the death had occurred more than an hour back, most probably due to a massive salient heart attack and gave the death certif cate, Further actions regarding the body to be was taken by the family.

Mrs. Baluja, by now, was coming back to her senses and was looking around her helplessly, so pathetic to see. Santanu called Indrani and together they went to their own f at. Santanu went to take a bath and asked Indrani to prepare tea. Then he went to attend the important meeting and told his wife "take care of Mrs. Baluja till her daughter arrives and they have to decide about further proceedings. I will come back to the meeting."

By the time Santanu came back around 4.30 P.M., the daughter Garima along with her husband and also their few relatives had arrived. The other daughter Manisha was to arrive from Pune by next day morning f ight. It had been decided to keep the body in the house till then, a huge ice block had been already ordered and the body kept over it to keep it cold.

Indrani had served tea and snacks to the entire household and had now come back to her f at, Bipasha and Partho had arrived from the school and a heavy pall of gloom hung over the entire atmosphere. It was Santanu's f rst close encounter with death and it had shaken him. He tried to watch some T.V. programme, could not concentrate and went out to the market.

Next day, Mrs. Baluja's other daughter Manisha arrived from Pune along with her husband and the body was taken to the Lodhi Road crematorium for the last rites. A hearse van had been called, the body laid on a bamboo ladder of sorts, was loaded on it and Santanu also went to the funeral along with the procession. Things had already been arranged, the body was laid on a wooden pyre and a nephew lit the f re and within two and half hours the body was reduced to ashes. There was no trace of Baluja, who had been his neighbour for more than two years. Death was the ultimate destination! He came back with a heavy heart.

Both Garima and Manisha stayed with their mother for a week and Manisha took her mother to Pune to stay with her for a few months. Mrs. Baluja left the key of the f at with Garima who assured her to take care of f at during her absence.

Both Bipasha and Kamlesh had f nished their class requirements for their second-year music course and Nandini said "you should now appear for the vocal, 2nd-year music examinations in Gandharva Mahavidyalaya at deen Dayal Upadhyay Marg near I.T.O junction. She arranged a date and Arora agreed to take them there. Lat year Santanu had taken them to the venue. The Gandharva Mahavidyalaya was a big three-storied building had a big campus. Various music courses – vocal, instrumental, western and classical dance classes were held there in different rooms and exams for various courses were also going on in other rooms. Bipasha and Kamlesh were asked to wait in a particular room on the second f oor where the various second-year exams were being held. Six students – both boys and girls were waiting in the room for their exams. In three hours, the exams for both were over. Results were to be communicated to their accredited teachers after about a week. Bipasha wanted to go for Medicine, so she was taking Brilliant Tutorials Postal tuition also. Both Kamlesh and Bipasha continued with their third-year music classes and Nandini informed them after a week that both had cleared their 2nd year exams and had to collect their certif cates from Gandharva Mahavidyalaya after two months.

-9-

A burglary had taken place in a f at during the night while its occupants were away on leave. Police were called, the night guards were warned for the dereliction of their duties. Santanu, as the Security- in-charge, instructed the guards to spend more time near the back side boundary wall areas, issued the night guards torches, whistles and lathis to carry out their duties more effectively. The burgled f at was adjacent to the back side boundary wall, about f ve feet in height behind which lied Jahapanah forest. Santanu along with some other members of the RWA went to the back side of Himadri apartments via the forest, to inspect the area and were surprised to see that the wall was only three feet high above the ground from one place on an elevated contour of the ground from where the thief could have scaled the wall. A few bricks were also kept there, one above the other from where the wall seemed to have been scaled and all of them felt the wall height had to be increased by at least three feet to make it safer for the residents. However, as the total length of the boundary wall was more than a hundred meters or so, a lot of expense was to be incurred for this work.

Another burglary took place within a week, again in a f at adjacent to the backside boundary wall and whose occupant also had gone on vacation. The Police felt that some insider must be providing the information and thus was in league with the miscreants. Police wanted all the maid servants, full time servants and others working inside the premises, to get their photo identity cards made after proper verif cations. President Agrawal called a resident's meeting in the evening during the weekend in the open space near the backside boundary wall on the west side. More than hundred residents attended the meeting which was a very good number considering the general apathy of the residents to get involved in running the day to day affairs of the RWA. The presence of a large number of ladies was another signif cant plus point as the ladies usually took no interest in the RWA affairs.

President Agarwal started by thanking the residents for attending the meeting to f nd a solution to this problem of theft. No sooner had he f nished, Mr. Nagpal, a retired resident, stood up and pointedly blamed the security-in-charge "he is an useless fellow. Instead of making periodic rounds around the f ats at night, he sleeps the whole night and indulges the security guards to be arrogant with the residents."

This was a pointed reference to the Miss Sudeshna Singh episode who had been forced to apologise to the guards. Santanu was stung and stood up. "I am also a resident paying equal maintenance charges every month and have to attend off ce every morning. I suggest Mr. Nagpal that since you are a retired person and have all the time at your disposal, take over my job. I am prepared to resign right away to give the reins of the job in your competent hands so that you can do the needful to stop burglaries at once" and threw a challenging look at him.

Mr. Nagpal was thrown off balance by such an aggressive posture and angrily retorted 'I have not been bitten by a mad dog to take up such useless jobs".

Santanu countered "that exactly is the point. It is very easy to criticise others but nobody is prepared to come forward to do some community service. We are all doing honorary service only and unless you are ready to come forward, please refrain from making such uncalled for comments."

Mr. Agarwal stood up "we have assembled here to f nd a solution and not to blame each other. All of you must remember that since nobody wanted the job inspite of my repeated efforts, I f nally could persuade Mr. Chakravarty to look after the security for which we are thankful to him. Let us talk to f nd a solution.

Mr. Malhotra stood up "Mr. President, please keep it in mind that we have elected you for the second time so that the RWA takes good care of us. We are regularly paying the maintenance charges. You cannot simply escape your responsibility when something goes wrong."

Agarwal corrected him "I was elected for the second term unopposed because the other candidate withdrew at the last moment but that apart, even if you publicly hang the President for the lapse, it may not prevent the burglary."

Mr. Nair, whose f at had been burgled now stood up "I suggest we should now come up with some concrete proposals so that such incidents do not happen in future" and everybody agreed with him.

Agarwal then requested the Secretary Bajaj to outline the f ndings of the Managing Committee. Bajaj stood up and began "The MC had a very detailed discussion for augmenting the security arrangements and has come up with three recommendations, which I would like to share with you." He looked at the audience.

He continued "It is very diff cult to patrol the whole premises effectively, covering all the four hundred and odd f ats at night with only two guards, as the other two guards have to remain at the two gates. We suggest that a team of three to four residents should volunteer their services to augment the nightly vigil, especially at the back sidewall area of each gate from around midnight to three P.M. for maximum burglaries take place, as per the police, during these three hours. The volunteers have to work on a weekly or fortnightly basis and police also feels that would be the best solution. To start with I am ready to volunteer and would like other residents also to come forward" and he looked at others.

Only Mr. Nair and Santanu volunteered for Gate No.1 area but inspite of repeated requests no other name came out. The President appealed "We have to take some responsibility for our own security so let us come forward to do some community service, I also offer my services for the Gate No. 2 area". He looked at the audience who remained totally unresponsive.

Bajaj continued "if this recommendation is not acceptable to the residents, then the only option is to employ two additional guards for the night shift and I hope the residents will have no objection for that" he looked up again.

This proposal found general acceptance and residents seemed enthusiastic, in unison they said "then go ahead" and some residents started to disperse.

Bajaj resumed "but for that to happen, the maintenance charges, have to be increased by ₹Ten per month per f at and I take it that you all are agreeable to that".

The sense of fragile consensus again seemed to dissipate by this pronouncement and the din of dissidence was audible from various quarters. Sharma stood up "we are already paying ₹Fifty per month, I say why can't you adjust it from the same amount?"

Nagpal commented "how can they? A good part of it must be reaching in their pockets?"

Subramanium, the treasurer stood up at this "All of you are welcome to the RWA off ce to scrutinize the account. We have eight security guards, four sweepers, one gardener, one electrician, one plumber apart from the common lightings, water charges and normal wear and tears, we are already in a hand to mouth situation and unless the subscription is increased there is no way to employ the additional guards. For better security you have to shell out more" and he sat down.

Finally, a decision was arrived to increase the maintenance charges with immediate effect and employ two additional guards for the night shift."

Bajaj, the Secretary was not yet f nished "One additional safety as suggested by the police and agreed by the RWA as necessary, is that the height of the entire, length of our boundary wall, especially   at the rear side facing the forest, has to be increased by at least three feet. We have inspected the wall from the forest side and found that at some places the height of the wall from the ground is hardly three feet and which can be scaled easily."

Mr. Das asked "what is the total length involved?"

Bajaj, after looking at his papers said "it is well over f fteen hundred meters covering all sides."

Grover enquired "and what would be cost implications?"

"Raising the front side may not be necessary and that would mean a little over a thousand meters. Raising the height with bricks may become too expensive but in Gangotri apartments they have constructed barbed wire fencing after installing angle iron pillars at every one metre distance. With the cost estimate based on their construction about a year back, the total cost of construction, would come to roughly ₹f ve hundred per f at. But the Gangotri people say it would be worth the expenditure."

The President wanted the views of the residents so that the job for additional safety could be undertaken after the collections are received. Some residents wanted to protest but the ladies came out strongly for the proposal and it was passed. It was decided that the residents would deposit the amount in RWA off ce preferably within two weeks. Mr. Bhatnagar, a civil engineer working with CPWD was made in-charge of the project along with secretary and Treasurer of the RWA as his team.

-10-

Partho had passed his high school with very good marks and had opted for the science stream. Indrani felt that he should try for I.I.T and with this idea got him admitted to the Brilliant Tutorials, its coaching classes being held in M Block market of GK-II. Bipasha and Kamlesh also passed their I.Sc with good marks and got admission in Gargi College of Delhi University in the South Campus. Bipasha wanted to study in the North Campus but Indrani felt that commuting to North Campus would take too much time and so Bipasha had to settle for Gargi college and Kamlesh also did the same. However, within a few months, both had to discontinue their Music IIIrd year classes as their practical classes stretched up to evening hours and that was the end of their music training.

Harish – the younger brother of Kamlesh, could not get admission in the regular classes of Delhi University due to insuff cient marks and had to settle for B.Sc (Pass) course in the evening classes in Deshbandhu College at Kalkaji. His one friend had got admission in B.Sc (Agriculture) at Solan in Himachal Pradesh and was studying there. He advised Harish also to join the college and so next year he applied there, got admission in B.Sc (Ag) and went to Solan. Manish had cleared his MBA, his passport was ready and he was waiting for his visa to USA. Priyanka also had cleared her exams and was now in 2nd year of her engineering classes.

Mrs. Jose lived on the top f oor and used to dry her washed clothes by spreading on her drying lines on the roof during morning hours. Before dusk, she used to go to the roof again to collect the dry clothes. Lately, she was feeling uneasy and complained to Indrani "last evening after dusk I went to the roof to collect the dry clothes and noticed that some boys and two girls were sitting in a corner and drinking and a boy trying to kiss the girl."

Indrani asked, "do you recognise any of them?"

"Yes, one of the boys was Manish and one girl seemed to be Juneja's daughter – that mod looking slim girl with sleeveless tops".

Indrani informed Santanu of the developments and the next day he along with Agrawal and Bajaj went to the roof and confronted the party.

Agrawal straightway charged them "this place is not meant for drinking and partying, what are you doing here?"

The boys were caught off-guard. One of them sheepishly told "we are having a small celebration tonight as Manish has passed his MBA."

Santanu countered "I understand you are meeting here regularly over a drink."

One of the boys protested "How do you know?" "because we are watching you for quite some time."

Agrawal asserted "listen! We are taking a liberal view this time and would let you off if you promise not to gather here anymore, otherwise, as President of the RWA, I will not only have to inform your parents but will also have to take deterrent action."

Bhatnagar's son protested "but we are not creating any nuisance and also doing it very quietly in a secluded place so as not to disturb anybody."

Secretary Bajaj chipped in "however, the majority of people are still against drinking in public and rooftop happens to be a public place. If you are so keen about drinking, you can have the party in your own home."

Manish replied, "our parents would not allow."

Agrawal said, "that is the point, don't create bad precedents, other residents especially the ladies don't approve of such practices and as President, I have to protect their interests also."

Juneja's daughter came up with the defence "Uncle, we are spending our own money and are not taxing anybody else."

Agrawal was quite f rm "that does not justify what you are doing and we all will be happier if this party is dissolved without any more fuss."

The boys looked at each other and slowly dispersed.

Next day the President put up a general notice on the RWA notice board:

It has been observed that some grown-up children of the residents are using the roofs for drinking sessions etc. after dark. As a preventive measure, all the doors of the roofs of every block will henceforth be locked in the evenings and the key would remain with the resident living on the top f oor. Residents are requested to co-operate.

Sd–
President

Anand returned from Bombay this time after almost four months. His family in the meantime was facing great f nancial diff culties and Mrs. Anand was forced to borrow from her parents to keep the household running. After returning from Bombay, Anand was not in his old cheerful disposition. There was another big quarrel with his wife. After about a month he went back to Bombay. Divetia tried to open up Anand several times but he was evasive and maintained a stoic silence which others interpreted as his deteriorating f nancial circumstances.

-11-

Mrs. Pahuja had gone to Bhopal to spend a week with her husband. While there, Aparna noticed that her husband, being alone, had taken to drinking in a big way. He had engaged a good looking young maid for cooking and doing daily chores and she suspected that Pahuja must be using her services in the bed also by the proprietary way she behaved. The maid also did not seem to be very pleased to see Aparna, unnecessarily interfering with her routine. Pahuja was gaining weight also and Aparna discussed his return to Delhi as he was almost completing two years in Bhopal. But Pahuja dashed all her hopes and said: "I have tried my best through a source but my bosses are not prepared to take me back at Delhi."

Aparna was concerned "does it mean that we have to stay separately till your retirement?"

Pahuja nodded gloomily "At present, it looks like that only."

Aparna's concern was justif ed from another angle also. After Pahuja was transferred, their income level also had gone down considerably. Apart from maintaining double establishment, they had also to send money to Nitin – their son in England who had one more year to f nish his studies besides the expenses for Priyanka's engineering studies. Aparna's interior decorator job was only for show and did not derive any regular income. Even after retrenching her full-time maid cum cook, she was hard-pressed to meet all the expenses. On top of it, Nitin had asked for a substantial amount of money as his examination fee to be paid by this month. Pahuja said "I will take a loan from the off ce to meet this contingency but we have to cut down our expenses further. They have not made me stores-in-charge here and thus there is no extra income also" he looked at his wife.

Aparna thought for a while and said "the only way out of this tight situation that I can see, is to send Priyanka to the hostel, rent out our Delhi f at and me coming to stay here with you. That way we could pay for our children's education without dipping into our savings."

Pahuja also could not think of any better alternative and had to agree for this. It was decided that Priyanka should try for a hostel seat and move out if it was available and after two months when he would come to Delhi on a month's leave, they would arrange to rent out the f at and both would shift here with bag and baggage. He asked Aparna to get in touch with brokers about renting out the f at in the meantime. Aparna went back to Delhi.

Mrs. Baluja had come back after spending three months with her younger daughter in Pune. She felt happy to come back to her environments and face the circumstances. Garima came and stayed with her for a fortnight and saw to it that all papers and f nancial matters of her mother were in order. She also took her mother to banks etc for handling the various f nancial and other transactions. She also persuaded Mrs. Baluja to learn driving as the car was there anyway and driving would give her mobility and independence which she would need if she wanted to stay alone. Mrs. Baluja started taking driving lessons and in three months was able to drive around the neighbourhood. But as she could not yet drive freely and with full conf dence, Garima sat beside her and took her out to the main roads to meet the full traff c and also for driving at night time and in another three months time Mrs. Baluja gained the conf dence to move around freely on the main roads.

Anju while playing in the evening told Bipasha in a whisper "my father has not yet come back from Bombay. We have not also heard from him since he left and for the last two months, he is also not sending any money. Mother is very unhappy and does not know what to do". Bipasha was shocked and told Indrani. Next day after coming back from school, Indrani along with Mrs. Baluja went to meet Mrs. Anand. After some small talks, Mrs. Baluja asked "when is Mr. Anand coming back?" and looked at her. This direct question took Mrs. Anand off guard. She hesitated for a while they could not control and started crying. Mrs. Baluja went to her, held her hands and said: "if anything serious has happened, you can conf de in us, may be we could help you in some way."

Mrs. Anand came out slowly, sobbing to her painful story. "For the last two years, I am seeing some change in him. He was earlier not like that. It all started after he started going to the Bombay off ce more frequently. Lately, he would f nd fault with me for no reasons, scold the children on small pretexts and was not taking any interest in household affairs, as if he was a guest here. For the last one year, he was sleeping separately and it seemed he had lost all the attractions for me. I was tolerating it for the sake of children and was maintaining a show of normal relationship in front of children but to tell you honestly, we were only staying under one roof and were barely in talking terms. Then he stopped giving me enough money for day to day expenses and for the last two months has stopped sending us any money. I have been a housewife all along, am not educated enough and don't know how to cope up with this situation or how to bring up the children all alone and am very worried about the future." Mrs. Baluja enquired "have you discussed with your parents?"

She said "Not yet, but they must have guessed something. I had married against their wishes." Mrs. Baluja said, "But I feel you should discuss with your parents at this stage." Mrs. Anand replied " I don't want to be a burden on them along with my children. My father is getting old, he is a small trader in Ajmal Khan market.

Mrs. Baluja enquired "what about your brother. Does he stay with your parents?"

"No, after his marriage two years back, he is assisting his father-in-law in running his handloom shop in Kalkaji, my bhabhi was not pulling on well with my mother and so last year they have moved out to her parent's big house in Kalkaji".

Mrs. Baluja asked, "that means your parents are living alone now?". "Yes", Mrs. Anand replied.

"Could you shift to their place and give this f at on rent so that it fetches you an independent regular income?" Mrs. Anand for the f rst time brightened up "I have to talk to them but can I give this f at on rent without his consent?"

Mrs. Baluja looked at Indrani who said " I will talk to my husband and let you know about it".

Mrs. Anand embraced Mrs. Baluja "that is the f rst ray of hope you have shown me in last one year or so. I have a premonition that our marriage is breaking up and I am so scared to think about the future and so much worried."

Mrs. Baluja asked the address of Anand's Delhi off ce from Mrs. Anand, which she could give by f shing out an old visiting card of Anand. Mrs. Baluja handed over the card to Indrani to f nd out about Anand by sending somebody from the RWA to his off ce and also take the address of his Bombay off ce from there. Indrani told Santanu about Mrs. Anand's plight and gave him Anand's card to f nd out more about the present whereabouts of Anand.

-12-

During the winter vacations, a major tragedy struck Kaul's family. Ritwick was by now freely driving the car independently. On Christmas night his one Christian school mate from Noida had arranged a party in his house and Ritwick along with his four friends from the neighbourhood decided to attend the party. Ritwick took permission from his mother and volunteered to take his car to go to Noida. There were great fun and frolic in the party including drinks and by the time party was over well past midnight, he and his friends were in a quite inebriated condition. While returning everybody was in a very festive mood and loud music was playing in the car stereo. It was a somewhat foggy night, Ritwick was driving and they were on the Nizamuddin bridge. In those days the bridge used to be only a two-lane each way and there was also no divider between going and coming lanes. Another bridge was being constructed side by side with Japanese assistance to make it wider for the increasing traff c. On a stretch of the bridge, some construction material was lying which left only one lane for driving with no room for overtaking. A slow-moving tempo was going from the left lane and the opposite side a heavily loaded truck was coming. In the fog coupled with his drunken state Ritwick could not properly judge the distance of the oncoming truck and accelerated to overtake the tempo. It was a miscalculation and in a split second his car collided head-on with the truck.

It turned out to be a very nasty collision. Nothing much happened to the truck except that it blocked one lane completely, but the front portion of the right side of the car was badly smashed due to the impact. There was a traff c jam, somebody called the police van and an ambulance was on the bridge. It took another half an hour to clear the jam and then the police van and ambulance reached the scene. They found the young driver spot dead with the steering wheel penetrating his chest, the windscreen was smashed, with the front and rear wheels and front doors jammed. Only the rear door from the other side of the car could be opened with much effort and one by one three bodies from the back seat were extricated, with one of them already dead and the remaining two still alive but bleeding profusely. One of them could still talk and gave the driver's name and telephone number. All of them were schoolboys and most probably underage to drive. Police immediately called the number. Sukriti was sleeping and took the phone eventually. Police informed her what had happened and asked her to send some male members immediately to the site to identify the dead and wounded.

It was well past three in the morning. Sukriti immediately rang Agrawal and in a dazed condition narrated what had happened. She also wanted to go but Agrawal f rmly said no to her. He woke up Bajaj and Pasricha and they left immediately after asking Sukriti to inform Kaul. What they saw was ghastly. The car was damaged beyond repair and had turned into a junk and a total loss. The wounded had been sent to the Safdarjung hospital, the two dead bodies including the boy sitting on the front seat were in a very badly mutilated condition and jammed in between the metals. It was not possible to take them out without cutting open the jammed metal doors, told the police. Agrawal identif ed the driver as Ritwick and Bajaj identif ed the other as Amit from Neelachal. A crane had been called to tow away the car to a workshop. The police assigned them the responsibility to inform Amit's parents and asked them to come to the Nizamuddin (East) police station in the morning by which time they hoped that the less wounded boy also will be able to give a statement.

Kaul reached by the morning f ight around noon and went immediately to the police station along with Pasricha, Kushwaha- Amit's father and Agarwal. By this time the dead bodies from the car had been extricated and were lying in the morgue of Safdarjung Hospital. After completing the formalities with police they went to Safdarjung Hospital and on seeing the mutilated state of the bodies of their sons both Kaul and Kushwaha decided that there was no point in taking the bodies to their homes. They decided to take the bodies straight to the crematorium at Lodhi Road after complying with the formalities with police and hospital authorities. By this time the third the dead body of Venkatesh Nair had also been identif ed by his father of, who had been informed by police to come to the hospital and was already there. Together they went to the crematorium and by the time they returned home, it was well past dark. Hrishikesh and Vincent were among the wounded, both were from Manas. Vincent was the lessor injured among the two and was discharged on the f fth day from the hospital whereas Hrishikesh who had two broken ribs and a fractured leg had to be in the hospital for two more weeks. All of them were from Delhi Public School, Mathura Road and Vincent had stated to Police that they had gone to Noida to attend a Christmas Party where liquor also had been served. Interestingly the parents of Hrishikesh and Venkat did not even know where their sons had gone. The incident was reported in the papers, one T.V. Channel showed the accident site along with the smashed car. The printed media, however, was not very charitable and some of them squarely blamed the parents for allowing their minor children to drive the car freely. Such accidents were on the rise in Delhi with increasing levels of prosperity and the police appealed the parents to exercise some control over their growing children or face the consequences.

Kauls lost their only son at such a young age and were very much grieved. However, though Ritwick was gone, troubles still followed the Kaul household. Immediate worry was that Ritwick was underage and did not have any driving licence, on top of it alcohol had been found in the blood of the victim and drunken driving was an offence. Kaul was also implicated being the father and it was his responsibility to refrain the son from driving as the car was registered in his name. He was very depressed sitting in the society off ce. Agrawal and Bajaj were consoling him but he was not convinced and said "See! this is the curse of modern life, the children drive the car and enjoy but when something goes wrong the parents have to bear the consequences. My one contact has requested the S.H.O. to hush up the case and he is demanding `twenty-f ve thousand as consideration fee. Not only that, the insurance company would pay no compensation as drunken driving by a minor has been established. The loss also means that Sukriti and my daughter have immediately to make some alternative arrangement for commuting to the school. He moaned aloud "I am in a great f x and am feeling very miserable".

Agrawal and Pasricha both advised him "whatever happened, has already happened. The loss is irreversible, but try to hush up the case soon, if possible negotiate, but settle it immediately. You are on the wrong side of the law and if the matter goes to the court, the lawyers would f eece you further and the case would linger".

Kaul paid up the hush money, settled the case and then went back after two weeks. Sukriti made arrangements to avail the school bus facility and the routine was restored minus their son.

Mrs. Anand had shifted to her parent's house in Karol Bagh after giving the f at on rent. Santanu found out that Mr. Anand had closed the Delhi off ce and operated from Mumbai.

-13-

Dr. Jai Shankar Prasad Tripathi was the Chief Medical Off cer of the hospital of the Ordnance Factory in Armapura, Kanpur and had been provided with a company bungalow within the township. His wife Jaya was a teacher in the Ordnance factory school and they had two sons Gautam and Saurav studying in class eleven and class seven in the Armapura School where their mother was teaching, both were very brilliant students. Before joining in Kanpur Dr. Tripathi was Medical Off cer in the Civil Hospital in Meerut. He hailed from village Khatauli nearby in the Meerut district and had completed his medical studies from Agra Medical College. Gautam passed his High School as well as I.Sc. in the f rst division, did his B.Sc. again in f rst division from Christian College and thereafter joined B.Tech. in Bio-Chemical Technology at local Harcourt Butler Technological Institute. After B.Tech he joined Delhi I.I.T. for his Ph.D. in Bio-Chemical Engineering and thereafter proceeded to university of Wisconsin, Madison campus in USA on a Post Doctoral fellowship (P.D.F.).

His younger brother Saurav also passed his High School and I.Sc. in the first division, cleared the all U.P. Pre-Medical Test (PMT) at the first attempt, joined Kanpur Medical College and decided to become a Surgeon. During his internship, his elder brother Gautam returned from USA to get married to Suman in an arranged marriage and returned to Madison with his wife. Saurav wanted to specialize in neuro Surgery and joined Master of Surgery (M.S.) in the same Medical College. When he was in the second year of M.S. Dr. Jay Shankar Prasad Tripathi retired from service, he had already purchased a flat in Kanpur near Gumti No.5 and settled there. Jaya continued in the school for three more years and thereafter she also retired.

Dr. Gautam after completing three years in the University of Wisconsin got an offer for P.D.F. from Stevens Institute of Technology in New Jersey. Suman by now was pregnant and before joining the new assignment he escorted her to Kanpur to his parents on a one month vacation, got some renovations done in their parent's f at and thereafter left to join the new assignment at New Jersey. Suman delivered a son in due time and after six months Dr. Gautam came for a short stay and returned with his wife and son to USA.

Dr. Saurav in the meantime was f nishing his M.S. and Jaya started looking for a match for his younger son. Saurav was quite friendly with several of his female colleagues but he was very f rm that he did not want to marry a doctor. From his own experience, he knew that doctors had very irregular duty hours, had emergency duties, night shifts and no f xed duty time. With this kind of life, he felt that one doctor was suff cient in a family and in order to balance his irregular and demanding job requirements, his wife had to be one with f xed duty hours and lighter workload, preferably a teacher may be, to take care of the household.

-14-

Indrani's closest friend in the School was Lopamudra Bhattacharya, the English teacher who was a few years older than her and who was a widow. Her husband was a professor in Delhi I.I.T. and had died of a heart attack at a relatively young age. She lived in their own house in Chittaranjan Park and was in the school for the last more than ten years since the death of her husband. Her children were in primary classes when their father had died and since then she was rearing them as a single parent. Her daughter Nilanjana had now grown into a beautiful lady studying in M.A. (Economics) in Delhi University, North Campus. Her son Indrani had passed out from Rajagiri School two years back and was now doing his B.Sc. from St. Stephens College.

Indrani's youngest brother Sushovan was coming on a one month's vacation in December after f nishing his Ph.D. in Bio-Chemistry from McGill University, Montreal in Canada, before joining Alembic - a well known pharmaceutical company in Montreal. He was to be in Delhi next month to spend four days with them and then proceed to Kolkata to their parents. The family was looking for a suitable match for Sushovan and Indrani was keen that he should also meet Nilanjana. She had already talked to Santanu about the match and he also had approved the idea. They planned a picnic during that time to Baikal lake in Faridabad on Sunday and invited Lopamudra and Samaddar's family also for the picnic. Mrs. Samaddar i.e. Soma was also her colleague, teaching in the same school and lived in G.K.-II. Samaddar was an executive engineer in Badarpur Thermal Power Station and had two daughters Bonnie and Dolly studying in class nine and class seven in D.P.S. Mathura Road.

It was decided that all the three families would cook one item each and all the families would assemble at the gate of Himadri Apartment at nine-thirty sharp. Lopamudra used to drive her own car and on the scheduled Sunday the three cars proceeded together via Tughlakabad fort, Shooting range, Surajkund from where a short cut road to Faridabad had come up recently. The picnic party reached Badkal lake by ten in the morning. It was a bright sunny day, though very cold. Many other families also had come and there was a festive mood all around. Santanu introduced others to Sushovan and they all sat together under the Sun. The f rst round of tea from a big f ask together with snacks were served by the ladies. After this Partho, Indranil, Bonnie and Dolly went away to play Badminton and rest of the group broke into small talks with each other, with old Bengali songs playing in the background on the cassette recorder.

Samaddar was narrating his dream of the last night "when I was in class seven or eight, we used to live in Asansol. We lived in a single-storeyed house, the roof of which was out of bounds for us as there was no staircase to the roof. But I used to climb on the roof surreptitiously at times by scaling the outer wall of the house and from there access a drainpipe to the roof, during the afternoons when everybody was asleep. Last night I saw that, as a boy, I had climbed to the roof of that house and was sitting there when somebody placed his right hand in a blessing pose on my head. I looked at him, he had a bluish body colour, was wearing a peacock feather on his temple and I recognized him as Krishna, the God of Mahabharat fame. I bowed at him, he blessed me and in the next instant disappeared." He looked around for effect and then continued "I was in sort of a trance and suddenly wide awake with a very satisfying feeling that I had received God's blessings."

Soma immediately protested "you did not tell me anything in the morning?" Samaddar said "I forgot in the hurry of getting ready in time". He then looked around "can anyone tell me what does this dream signify?"

Many different versions were given. Sushovan opined "may be because of His blessings to you as a boy, you have become what you are today".

"But then why this time lag in delivering the blessings to me so late in my life?"

Soma quipped "you better ask God Krishna for the answer" and everybody laughed. From there the discussions drifted on to the dreams. Santanu said," let us not try to f nd meanings in a dream, often it borders to being absurd but nothing to beat Indrani's dreams".

Sushovan got curious "what about it?" and then he looked at her mejdi. Santanu elbowed her "hey~ why don't you tell about it?"

Indrani was puzzled "which one?" Nilanjana jumped at it "Aunty, that means you have a whole collection of dreams, please tell us some of them."

Santanu gestured "wait, let me recollect" and then he turned to Indrani "that one about carrying the tree branch".

Indrani looked at Soma and Lopamudra "you remember Lopa, last year in commemoration of the world environment day, one Dr. Ahuja had been invited by our Principal and he had delivered a very thought-provoking lecture about the trees keeping the environment clean and had stressed about preserving the trees and greenery?" Soma said "yes! Yes! I remember". Lopa added, "and he had planted f ve trees around our playground, three of which have survived till now."

Indrani continued "I dreamt a few days later that due to some function in the school, I was held up till late in the evening and it was getting dark when I came out. I was in a hurry to reach home but no autos were available in the vicinity......"

Nilanjana interrupted her "but aunty, you live just across the road, why did you need an auto?"

Indrani agreed "but in my dreams, my home seemed far away and in my desperation, I started walking toward Chittaranjan Park. After crossing Neelachal I suddenly noticed a small branch of a tree lying on the road. I immediately caught hold the severed end of it, tried to lift it on my shoulders, could not and then dragged it back to the school, went straight to the Principal and deposited the branch in his custody. Father Thomas very much appreciated the gesture and instructed me to count the number of sub-branches together with the number of leaves in each sub-branch and noting down the details in the School register after taking due care that the leaves did not receive any injury during handling. In all seriousness, very meticulously, I noted down the details in the school register, satisf ed that I had done a good job and by the time I came out it was midnight".

Soma asked, "how did you reach home and why the school remained open till midnight?"

Santanu replied, "that was outside the scope of the dream."

Lopamudra began "may be six or seven years back I had seen a very scary dream. Nilu was studying in school those days and my parents were staying with me".

Nilanjana asked, "Ma, have you told us about it?" "No, but now I am telling" and then she started" After some stay back in the school, I was coming down from the second f oor, descending from the main staircase. All the students were also gushing out in their mad rush to get out f rst. While descending the f ight of stairs I noticed after a while that it seemed to have an unending number of stairs and though I was continuing to descend no sooner I cleared one set, another f ight of stairs came into view, I had to start once again and I was very tired by the exercise, "she looked around and continued "those of you who have visited Vaishno Devi shrine on top of the hill, would remember that while returning, instead of following the long circuitous road going down, there is also a short cut by going down the f ight of stairs straightway. To start with, it looks easy but after going down and down for more than half an hour your calf muscles start aching and you feel exhausted. Right after our marriage, I had gone there once along with my husband and was dead tired by the time we reached Katra via the staircase route. I was experiencing the same feeling while coming out of school in my dreams". Samaddar quipped "very interesting! May be Vaishno Devi was calling you again, Jai Mata di!" and with folded hands, he touched his forehead. Nilanjana was curious "but there is nothing so scary about it?"

Lopa resumed "going down and down, after some time I noticed that I was the only person left, all others had gone, it was dark and there was an uncanny silence all around. I was scared and could not also see properly but I had no choice and had to continue. I was heavily panting and sweating profusely but could not stop. After an interminable time which seemed like an eternity, ultimately the f ight of stairs came to an end and I reached somewhere. In the dead of night and in the dim light it looked like some market place but totally strange to me. I felt completely lost, unable to recognize anything from the surroundings. It looked like a different city altogether with some small town like topography with single-storeyed small houses, cattle tied in their front yards and no multistoried buildings. I woke up with a start, very panicky and perspiring heavily. In a dazed condition, I looked around, slowly recognized my room and Nilu sleeping by my side. I felt so relieved to realize that it was only a dream."

Santanu now stretched the conversation further "Another interesting point about Indrani's dream is that while narrating the dream she goes into the minute details as if she has seen a movie. I often wonder how can she observe so many things in a dream but even more puzzling aspect is that if she is awake midway through a dream say for going to the toilet or to drink water, then after the break when she quickly falls asleep again she resumes the dream and continues with its remaining part as if it was an interval in a cinema show".

Everybody turned to Indrani "Come on! that is stretching a dream too far!! Do you want us to believe that?" Indrani, however, steadfastly defended seeing the dreams with one break "Don't think that I am bluff ng you. It has happened to me many times. It comes when you concentrate on your dream."

At this point, the group needed a break to stretch their limbs. Sushovan got up as he had an urge to smoke and wanted to go to some corner away from the sight of his elders. Bipasha and Nilanjana were talking while taking a stroll and he also accompanied them. From the corner of her eyes, Indrani observed her brother talking to Nilanjana and was happy. She reminded Bipasha "lunch would be served in half an hour, please bring Partho and all others in time."

After lunch Samaddar and Santanu lied down under the sun and took a nap. By the time they woke up, the singing session was in full swing and Soma was singing. It was followed by Nilanjana who was a good singer and then Sushovan requested Indrani and Santanu to sing a duet. While the singing session was progressing, Bipasha served tea and snacks to the group. By late afternoon they all returned with a day well spent.

After dinner at night, Sushovan was reading a book in his room when Indrani entered and sat on his bed "Khokon, how do you like Nilanjana?"

Khokon was Sushovan's his nickname in the family, replied "what do you mean by how do I like. She is all right," and looked at her. She teased him "Is it only all right or a little more than that. If you say so, I can talk to her mother about marriage?"

Sushovan blushed "I haven't thought about it."

"Then think about it. Ma is also looking for a match for you. Nilanjana is a nice girl, well educated and comes from a decent family. She would be a good match for you".

Sushovan said, "you can talk to mother about her also but I can marry only next year after I am settled in the job".

"that would enable her also to f nish her M.A. and should be O.K." and then pointedly asked, "should I talk to her mother then?"

Sushovan smiled "yes, you can".

Indrani was very happy "then I will ask them to come to us for tea some time before you leave for Canada. He agreed "as you think proper, but Ma also has asked me to see a few girls during my stay at Kolkata so any f nal decision can be made only after I return from there after a fortnight before returning to Canada via Delhi" and Indrani nodded.

-15-

Mrs. Baluja by now had been used to live alone. She was quite independent, used to freely drive around to meet her friends and relatives, had developed her social circle – mostly widows and single women who used to have periodic get-togethers also in each other's place. She had also joined the yoga classes in the park in the mornings and used to keep her busy outdoors in order not to feel lonely. After Baluja's death, the table tennis club of the block slowly lost its steam, children of the block also were losing their earlier enthusiasm for the game and the club started slowly disintegrating. The dinner gets together of the block also had become very irregular after his death as well as consequent to Anand's going and seemed very near to being abolished altogether.

Kaul had come back from Surat and the family was reunited minus of course Ritwick. Pahuja's Bhopal tenure was over but from there he was transferred to Lucknow. Priyanka had got accommodation in hostel and Mrs. Pahuja had moved to Lucknow along with her husband after giving their f at on rent. The barbed wire fencing work along the boundary walls of the RWA had been completed to the satisfaction of the residents and this had increased the overall safety of the premises from thefts. After three consecutive terms in RWA. Agrawal and his team got defeated and Juneja becomes the new President with Bhatia as secretary and Kaul as Security-in-charge.

Bipasha and Kamlesh had passed their B.Sc and were now studying in M.Sc previous in Delhi University North campus. Partho had passed I.Sc and had been able to clear I.I.T.J.E.E to secure admission in I.I.T Roorkee and left his house for I.I.T Roorkee hostel. Manish had got the visa and had left for USA on sponsorship from his sister in Philadelphia. His jijaji had lined up a job also for him in his f rm. Kamlesh had many admirers in her neighbourhood as well as in Delhi university as she was a pretty, fair-complexioned tall girl with a very amicable personality. However, she was of a serious type and her relationship with boys remained conf ned to a friendly but formal limit. Bipasha was her closet friend and they had a very good understanding by being friends for so many years. Both were progressing quite well smoothly through their student life without any diversions but suddenly Kamlesh found herself on an unexpected crossroad for which she was unprepared.

Marriage is a very important event in every girl's life and in Indian society, most of the marriages are still the arranged ones. Kamlesh was not only beautiful but her father was rich also. It was thus expected that she would be very decently married and she was reaching marriageable age. Arora family along with their children had gone to attend some marriage at Rohtak where Arora met his old friend from Ludhiana, one Mr. Sehgal who was now settled in Rohtak. Poonam and Simran also knew each other well and so both families met very warmly after more than f fteen years or so. Sehgal's son Prem, who was now an engineer in America, had returned home after eight years on a holiday for one month. Prem was a tall, handsome, smart young man well mannered and brimming with an easy self-conf dence which comes from doing well in life and was also a good conversationalist. Arora who was looking for a match for his daughter was very impressed with Prem, invited the Sehgal's for lunch next Sunday in Delhi. Sehgal's brother, who also had come to attend the marriage, it turned out, lived in Paschim Vihar and Prem said after this marriage he was going to stay with his uncle for a week and meet his friends in Delhi.

Prem did not want to return to India, was very critical of Indian ways and things by comparing with over there (USA). Sehgals came for lunch the next Sunday to Arora's house and their old friendship was renewed. While in Delhi Prem used to move around in taxis, spend his evenings in Oberoi and Ashoka hotels with friends and spent money very extravagantly. He visited Aroras also several times bringing lavish gifts for everybody. Punjabis in general, like to live with good material comforts and admire fast life. Arora, saw Prem as an epitome of a modern young man, ideal match for his daughter, guaranteeing her a happy life and Poonam also agreed with it.

In the 1990s in the Delhi's upper-middle-class societies, marrying your daughter to a well-established boy working in USA, was considered a highly coveted achievement, an 'in' thing so to say enabling you to climb up a few notches in your social standings and Arora did not want to miss this God-sent opportunity. He talked to Prem's parents during his next visit to Rohtak along with his wife and decided to marry Kamlesh with Prem. Sehgals also were very happy with this proposal as they also wanted to see their son settled down in life. As Prem was to return to USA in a fortnight, Aroras f xed the marriage date next week and informed Kamlesh as well as Prem accordingly, who was still in Delhi.

In his hurry and eagerness to have Prem as his son-in-law, Arora did not feel any necessity to check Prem's antecedents and was fully satisf ed that he had made a very good match. He called Harish from Solan. Kamlesh and Prem were married, which was solemnized in Ashok hotel and the married couple were sent to Manali on Honeymoon, sponsored by Arora. Sehgals returned to Rohtak with lots of dowry and expensive gifts. Prem went back to USA after a week, after assuring his parents, in-laws and the young bride that he would call her soon. Kamlesh lamented to Bipasha "everything happened so fast that I had no control on anything and I had to leave my studies also mid-way." However, everybody felt it was a small price to pay for such a coveted marriage.

-16-

The co-operative stores were running very successfully. Pasricha was devoting his spare time as well as his business acumen in running the stores and as a consequence, the stores had expanded its range of products, had been able to employ a manager and an accountant, on a part-time basis. Agrawal had donated a computerized billing machine with a result that the billing procedure had become much faster now as well as accurate and the earlier practice of manual billing had been discarded.

In USA Manish was staying with his sister Raashi and jijaji Arjun Grover in Philadelphia. Arjun had also arranged an entry-level temporary job for Manish within a few months of his arrival and so Manish was employed now. However, after six months in his job, he found out that his MBA from Modinagar would not help him in fetching a good job in US He discussed this problem with his jijaji also who had done his Masters in engineering from US. Manish said, "I feel my MBA is of no value here and thus I cannot aspire for a good future with this degree".

Arjun agreed "that was my dilemma also when I had come here with an engineering degree from Ambala and then I had done my masters here. I believe if you wanted to stay on in this country, it would be better to acquire a degree from some US university."

Raashi added, "though you will f nd it very tough if you go here for a professional degree, but the effort would be a good investment for your future." Manish agreed with their assessment but he did not want to go for another MBA. He felt if he had to go for a degree, he would likc to do something else and made a mental note to look for some f eld which had a high demand.

***

Prem had done his engineering from Rohtak and had come to USA to do his masters in engineering from Syracuse University. He had applied for immigration and got the immigration visa. He, however, failed several courses, could not f nish his masters and had to quit. He managed to get a job at a lower level with an engineering f rm working in Alaska and was working there since. He had married an American girl, a waitress working in a bar and this had helped him in getting the citizenship also in due time. Thus after eight years in the country, he was now a US Citizen. He had not told about his failure to get a US degree as well as his marriage to his parents also. His f rm had sent him to Syracuse on a temporary assignment of about six months or so after he came back from leave to India. Kamlesh was a beautiful girl and since Mr. Arora was so keen, Prem could not resist marrying his daughter. Nobody asked him anything and he also did not tell. He found that people in India were hankering to get their daughters married to anybody settled in America and so he also went along with the misadventure just to have a good time while in India.

He was now in Syracuse, his wife was working in New York, but used to come to him during weekends and so he had taken a one-bedroom apartment while retaining his New York apartment also. Since Syracuse was his known place, he had studied here, he had friends also and use to socialize among the Indian community along with his wife Cynthia. He was now in a big problem, Kamlesh was writing him letters, so far f ve letters had come, asking him to expedite her coming to USA but he had not replied a single letter because he did not want her to come. This type of duping was not an isolated incidence, in Punjab there were hundreds of cases where the young men working in US or UK used to come home on vacation and marry some girl of unsuspecting parents, have good time while in India and then leave for good, after ruining the girl's whole future, who had to be sacrif ced on the altar of their parent's greed for NRI sons-in-laws.

Manish had ultimately zeroed in computer graphics as an emerging f eld in great demand. He discussed with Arjun who endorsed him but had some doubts "I don't know your background in computers but can only tell you that you have to be quite computer savvy even at your entry-level".

Manish admitted "I have handled computers only during my MBA."

"then I would advise you to join some entry-level computer course at the university and in the meantime practice on my computer at home daily for some time."

Manish agreed and joined some entry-level crash courses in the university of Philadelphia along with practising daily on P.C. at home. In a few months, he gained the competence and then applied for masters programme courses in computer graphics from the next session in the university.

<h1 style="text-align:center">-17-</h1>

It was more than three months since Prem had gone back but Kamlesh had not received a single letter from him in spite of having written f ve letters. Thereafter Sehgal wrote a strong letter to his son to reply to his newlywed wife's letters and say something def nitive about her coming. The reply came after a fortnight in the form of a short letter to Kamlesh, which read:

Dear Kamlesh,

I have made a big mistake by marrying you. I am living in this country for long and have certain responsibilities. After I fulf l my obligations, I would be in a position to call you but you will have to wait till then.

–Prem

Kamlesh showed the letter to his in-laws who also were equally baff ed. Nothing was written about the kind of responsibilities which prevented him from calling his wife there. His brothers and sisters were married. Mr. Sehgal was in his own business and was doing well and could not think of any liability of his son. At this stage, Aroras visited Rohtak and took their daughter home. Kamlesh showed this letter to Bipasha and conf ded "my parents are very worried and so I have not shown this letter to them. I cannot fathom what the responsibilities could be "and she started crying with big teardrops falling from her eyes. Bipasha was very concerned and felt "there appears to be something very f shy about the whole thing. My instinct tells me, though I would feel very happy if I am proved wrong, that after living in America for such a long time he may have developed some intimacy with some girl over there and is perhaps unable to come out of it", she looked at her friend, who though crying all the while said "that is also what my worst

56

fears are and I am very unhappy with my parents that they got me married me in such a hurry, without even bothering to check anything about his antecedents."

Bipasha asked her "what do his parents say at Rohtak?"

They also are unaware of his activities there and know about him only what he has told them."

Bipasha consoled her "Anyway since now you have become his wife, you have to f nd out the truth for your good and after long deliberations, they agreed to a draft letter to be sent to him:

"Received your short note but was very disappointed to go through it as it happened to be your f rst letter after marriage. You have not mentioned anything about why do you consider marriage as a mistake. If you have developed any liaison with any girl over there and are unable to sort out the matter, I am ready to help you. However, I would very much like to know how much time you would take to get over the obligations that you have mentioned you have and also what should I do in the meantime. I am feeling very lonely and people have started talking about your inability to call me, there. Your parents are also not favourably inclined with your reluctance. I would sincerely wish that you call me at the earliest and yes I am now staying with my parents in Delhi, so please reply at this address."

***

Reema, the youngest daughter of Agrawal, had come to her parents for her second delivery. She was staying with her in-laws in Dehradun as her husband was in the army and was posted in a non-family area in Kashmir. Her f rst son Sonu was now four years old and her parents were very happy to see their grandson. Nandini was still continuing with her music tuition classes and had recently won the best teacher award from South Delhi from the Gandharva Mahavidyalaya. Six of her students had f nished their f ve-year music course, her students were consistently performing very well in the music exams and some of them had become music teachers in the schools. Nandini had given a party to the mothers of her ex-students and Poonam and Indrani were also invited. After others had left and only Poonam and Indrani were there, she asked Poonam "how is Kamlesh?" She knew that Kamlesh had still not gone to US.

Poonam moved closer to her "I don't know whether we have committed a mistake by getting her married in such a hurry but it seems Prem is not interested to call her over there. What do you advise us to do at this stage?"

Nandini had married three daughters and so could give some helpful suggestions, Poonam thought. Nandini thought for a while and said: "I feel you should frankly talk to her in-laws as they are the only people who could exert some pressure on their son but before that ask Kamlesh also about her feeling?"

Poonam lamented "that is the problem, she does not share her feelings in the matter with us at all and evades whenever we want to bring the subject to her."

Nandini suggested "may be Bipasha would know something, what do you say Indrani?"

Indrani replied "I had asked her but she only said that may be Prem has a past but beyond that, she was not ready to tell anything about her best friend's problems, but she is very upset about the whole affair. May be you should talk to Sehgals as Nandini suggested and sooner the better" she looked at Poonam.

No reply came for the letter Kamlesh had written to Prem, two more letters also remained un-replyed. One day Poonam asked her about Prem and Kamlesh broke down and told about the only letter she had received from Prem and showed it to them. Arora was very upset and the next day they went to Rohtak and talked to Sehgals about Prem's intentions. They were also very concerned with their son's attitude and promised to talk to Prem and let them know in a few days. Next day Sehgal telephoned Arora that he had talked to his son and Prem has asked him to send Kamlesh. Her passport was already there as two years back Aroras had gone to Hong Kong on a holiday. Arora had already applied for her visa and as soon as it was available, they sent Kamlesh to USA Arora gave Kamlesh $100 extra to open a separate bank account in her name after reaching there so that she could transact money independently and if necessary he could also send her some money. Both families went to the airport to see her off and hoped that ultimately her troubles were going to be over soon. She boarded on an Air India f ight for New York and Sehgal phoned Prem to pick her up from the airport at New York.

Bipasha was in M.Sc f nal year by now and Indrani was looking for suitable match for the marriage but Bipasha wanted the marriage plans to be postponed by a few years as she wanted to do her Ph.D. Hot exchanges followed between mother and daughter but Indrani persisted "this is the right age for marriage Baby for as you grow older and your qualif cations increase, your suitability in the marriage market will go on decreasing."

Bipasha retorted "I am not a commodity for sale in a market place. I want to be f nancially independent and so I want to pursue Ph.D, marriage or no marriage."

Santanu at this point intervened and reasoned with her from another angle "see, we are also getting older and I would retire in about three years. As a father, I would like to see you well married and settled before I retire."

Bipasha, however, was in no mood to yield "Kamlesh also was married in time, I am sure her parents also intended well at that time but see what happened." Indrani admitted partly "Anyway, now that she has gone there, let us hope things will be O.K. there."

Bipasha countered "but if it doesn't?"

Indrani rebuked her "let such thoughts not even cross our minds, let us all hope and pray that her bad days would soon be over."

Bipasha struck a deal ultimately with her parents "look! I will appear for the qualifying exams for Ph.D after my f nal year results are out and if I can't make it then you can go ahead with your boy hunt."

Santanu said "fair enough."

Bipasha further clarif ed "All I am saying now is to give me one more year before you start looking for a match and yes! Strictly NO to any NRI boy".

Her parents agreed.

***

Bhatnagar and Sarin had a big quarrel. It had so happened that Bhatnagar's son Aashish and his friends were playing cricket. Sarin's f rst-f oor house was facing the park and one of the hits from Aashish or the team had broken the big glass pane of his door facing the park. He had conf scated the cricket ball and had refused to give it to the boys. There were hot exchanges and Sarin complained to Bhatnagar.

"This is the third time. I am sick of getting it repaired every time for no fault of mine. I can give the ball only after they promise not to play in this park and pay the repair cost."

Bhatnagar said, "you settle with the boys, don't drag the parents into it."

Sarin was furious "the parents have to take some responsibility of the misdeeds of their children."

Bhatnagar slammed the door on his face "I have nothing to do with this."

Sarin made a written complain to Juneja, the President of RWA and Sarin, Bhatnagar as well as Aashish were called to the off ce. Sarin's plea that playing cricket in the park should be banned, could not be accepted as the boys said "Uncle, there is no other place to play" and others also agreed that the boys should be given some space for playing and outdoor activities. They were ultimately made to promise that thereafter they would not play with a cricket ball but use a tennis ball instead. Bhatnagar and Sarin were requested to share 50% of the cost each, this time and the dispute was settled.

-18-

Sushovan, on his way back from Kolkata, made a stopover in Delhi for two days. Indrani invited Lopa for tea and Nilanjana and Sushovan were sent to the balcony to talk to each other alone. He had seen a few girls in Kolkata but he had told his mother also that he felt Nilanjana was the best among them. His mother had asked him the reason. He said, "I can't pinpoint really but somehow it seemed to me that the parents and the girls here had already presumed that I have settled down there permanently and the girls were more thrilled with the prospect of living in Canada."

His mother asked "what is wrong with their presumption. Most of the boys who go there don't come back."

Sushovan said, "I would like to keep the choice open for some more years as I have not yet made up my mind."

His mother had only said "Anyway, after meeting the girl again in Delhi, you let your choice be known to Indrani, as I don't want to give false hopes to these girl's parents" and he agreed.

Indrani had conf ded to Lopa "he has not liked any girl at Kolkata and wants to see Nilanjana again, so please come for tea to my place today" and Lopa had agreed. She told Indrani "without my husband, I was very worried about her marriage but I would be very thankful to you if this materializes."

Nilanjana had liked Sushovan, though she had a small hitch and she decided to convey it while talking to him in the balcony. After some small talks, she came to the point "my father died when I was hardly seven years old and since then mother has brought us up as a single parent, devoting her whole self in giving us a decent life and good education. She would retire within a few years. She is very independent by nature and would live alone. I would like to live near her so that I could look after her if such a time comes. I know that you will have a very bright future, I cannot expect any better match than you but still..."

Sushovan looked at her eagerly "but... what...?

"Please don't take it as my audacity but if you settle down in Canada, I will be very far from my mother and that is why I feel I am not the right girl for you." and looked at him apologetically.

He said "In that case, after retirement, can she not come to stay with us?"

She shrugged "No, that won't happen." He was puzzled "how do you know?"

"because my father was an engineer working in London when they got married and they lived for two years in England, then my mother persuaded him to return to India."

Sushovan smiled "So, it runs in the family?"

"May be"

"What was your father doing after coming back?"

She replied, "He was Associate Professor in I.I.T Delhi". Sushovan could only say "Humm! I am impressed."

She continued "with your credentials, I am sure you will f nd many girls quite eager to settle down in Canada and I only hope that you won't laugh at the sentiments of a silly girl."

Sushovan remained silent, kept looking at her for a long time till she felt embarrassed and looked the other way, then he held her both the hands and f nally said.

"Done! So it is f nally settled."

She looked puzzled "what is settled, I don't get it?"

"that we will also come back to India provided you agree to marry me. The only point of contention still open for discussion remains, if yes, would you allow me a grace period of a few years time over there, suff cient to f nd a suitable job in India?" "he looked at her."

She shyly cast her eyes down "who am I to do anything with your decision making. It has to be your own free and independent decision, to be or not to be in India."

He said, "but I have already made my decision."

She looked at him "what decision?"

"that you are the right choice for me" he smiled and pressed her hand.

He continued "you know Nilanjana, in fact, I am very thankful to you for enabling me to make my decision for coming back. I have a very good job waiting for me on my return but now it means I will not take up that job."

She looked up questioningly "then what will you do?"

"I will have to take up some post-doctoral fellowship in some good institution for a few years which will add to my qualif cations for some university teaching position here. Are you agreeable to this change of plan?

She said "you know much better than me as to what is good for your career."

"But I want you to be there with me, right after you f nish your M.A."

"For that, you will have to talk to my mother" she smiled.

He stood up "so, that settles everything, any more questions?" "No, not from my side."

"then wait for a few seconds. I will bring my camera and will take a few snaps of yours." After the photo session, they exchanged addresses and then went back together to the waiting elders. He took a few more snaps and then broke the news. Next day he went back.

-19-

On reaching JFK airport in New York, Kamlesh was very disappointed to f nd that Prem had not come to the airport to receive her as assured by her father-in-law. However, as she had already made a foreign trip with her parents to Hong Kong some time back, she could negotiate the diff culty of changing over to the domestic terminal with some assistance from the airport staff, boarded the Syracuse f ight and telephoned him to come to the airport there but he was not at home.

On receiving his father's call Prem was quite disturbed. He could not think of any more excuses for delaying the coming of Kamlesh and so gave his consent for sending her. But this meant some immediate adjustments had to be made. He telephoned Cynthia, whom he had not told anything about his marriage in India, that from now on he would visit her in New York on weekends and the following weekend when he was to visit New York, he put all her belongings in his car and cleared the house of her belongings. He reasoned with himself that since he had to spend only a few more months in Syracuse before he was transferred back to the New York off ce and onwards to Alaska he had to manage this end for few months only and then he would disappear. He could foresee that his parents back home as well as Kamlesh would be hurt by his decision but he had no choice. Cynthia could do him much more damage than Kamlesh and so Kamlesh had to be sacrif ced to save his skin in his adopted country.

Prem did not turn up at the airport even at Syracuse. Kamlesh felt very helpless being all alone in a new country and being thus unwelcomed. Anyway, boarding a taxi, she reached at the designated address. He was very much present in the house but gave some lame excuse for not being able to come. Moreover, he did not also show any warmth which is natural when a newly married husband meets his wife after a long separation. Anyway f nally she was reunited with her husband and she thanked God for it. She telephoned her in-laws and parents of her safe arrival and started living together with Prem but somehow he did not seem to be the same old Prem.

Kamlesh gradually found out that Prem used to remain very aloof. Her romantic dreams of married life were getting shattered as the days passed due to the neglect and callous behaviour of her husband. On top of it he used to leave for New York every Friday evening and returned only on Monday mornings. He was supposedly in a good job, earned well but was very stingy in the matter of giving money to her, as a result, she used to always remain in a tight position.

An Indian Sindhi family used to live on the third f oor. Gradually she came to know Mrs. Asrani who was a middle-aged woman. Her husband was a businessman and she was living in the town for the last ten years or so. She went to the bank one day and with her introduction opened an account in her name by depositing hundred dollars given by her father. Mrs Asrani had two school-going children and once in a while, she used to go to her apartment when Prem was not there because he did not like her making friends with anybody.

Prem's lavish lifestyle in Delhi was in sharp contrast to his present way of living, he had metamorphosed almost into a different person. He never used to take her on outings, nor used to much talk to her, used to come late from off ce on weekdays and was absent on weekends. Kamlesh used to remain conf ned to her house all day and alone. She was suffocating, all joy was sadly missing and had gone out of her life, she felt very helpless and dissatisf ed with what the life had offered to her. She did not also want that people back home should know about the miserable life that she was leading here and so she stopped writing letters home, neither she discussed over the phone, her circumstances to anybody.

After three months or so of leading such a miserable life, she wanted to face Prem and wanted to ask him why did he marry her if he could not give her a better life. She was also fed up with his going away to New York alone with almost a religious zeal every weekend without any fail and without telling her any reason for it. She decided to confront him when he came back late from his off ce on Wednesday and asked point blank "you have to tell me why do you go to New York every weekend without fail and if your going is so necessary, I would also accompany you this time" and gave him a challenging look.

Prem was silent for a few seconds by the impact of this direct attack and then weighed his answer mentally. His tenure in Syracuse was coming to an end. He was expecting a letter from New York off ce to return to his parent off ce within a day or two and so this was the right time to get rid of her. He was ready for a f ght.

Prem looked at her and then coldly asked "you wanted to know the truth as to why I go to New York every week and so I will tell you – I go because my American wife lives there and we have a three-year kid also. Are you satisf ed now? And no you are not welcome there" and returned her challenging look.

Kamlesh was stunned. She was suspecting some affair for long but this arrogant declaration as if stabbed her and she became not only speechless for a while but also sort of paralyzed. How can he be such a crook? He played a con game with her knowingly and destroyed her whole life. Then she burst out, she welled up anger of these months f nding an outlet at last "you mean fellow, you cheated me, my parents, as well as your parents knowingly? You breached the trust off all of us including your own parents and your wife as well. Have you no conscience at all?

This slapping of charges led to a big quarrel. Prem also f ared up "I did not ask for your hand. Your father only came running to my parents with the idea of marriage."

"but if you were an honest man, you should have said at that time that you are already married?" She retorted.

"Nobody asked me and your father was dying to get an NRI son-in-law and I simply obliged him. He ought to have the good sense to verify my antecedents independently "he shrugged. She shouted back "how dare you to talk about my father in such a way? He did not know at that time that he was dealing with a crook"

"whatever! But you are the person who is going to suffer for his indiscretion. O.K. I won't talk about your father but do you happen to remember that I did not ask you to come here. Only you were repeatedly pestering me through your letters to allow you to come?"

"I did not know at that time that it was only a fake marriage for you. I could not even imagine that somebody can be so. so..." She fumbled for an appropriate word.

Prem countered "Anyway, so now you know the truth."

She started crying "O God! Now, what shall I do?"

He curtly said "that is your problem" he stood up abruptly, went to the bathroom and bolted the door from inside.

Kamlesh sat there for some time with her head between her two hands then went to bed and bolted the door from inside. She did not want to share her bed anymore with him, she hated him with all her heart. She had become a victim of circumstances, no the bad judgment of her father. She kept thinking that he had told the truth about his father's hankering after NRI son-in-law and could not sleep for the whole night. Tears were falling from her eyes and she was sobbing silently all alone. This sham marriage had destroyed her. Her whole world had collapsed before her and not only that, she had been catapulted to this new world because of this marriage where she is a total stranger, has no support system, did not know also what to do but she hated to be with this man any more. Why fate had played such a prank with her? What had she done that she was being so severely punished? She was in a sort of delirium from self-pity and didn't know when she had fallen asleep.

In the morning she got up late. It was already eight-thirty. She opened the door and looked around not knowing how to face him but fortunately, he had already left for off ce. She was hungry, prepared breakfast and went on with the daily chore. She could not yet muster the courage to tell her parents. She was also very ashamed to tell about her such a pitiable state. Her self pride prevented her from opening her heart to anyone.

Prem went to the off ce, phoned his New York off ce and by evening received a fax message, requesting the Syracuse off ce to release him by Friday, so that he could join the New York off ce on Monday. At night he returned to his house, did not talk to Kamlesh who also showed no inclination to talk to him. They slept in separate rooms and on Friday morning he left for his off ce early, came back in the evening, packed all his baggage, put it in his car, and after clearing his room left for New York, leaving a note on his table that the lease of the apartment was to expire in a month.

Kamlesh could not sleep on Friday night and kept thinking about her future. His note about the house meant she could only stay there for one more month and his clearing all luggage meant he was not coming back anymore. She was almost getting sick with anxiety for her future and was in a deep depression. Towards early morning she fell asleep and dream about her childhood that she and Bipasha were running in the garden of Lady Irwin Primary school at Defence Colony, holding their hands in a very carefree manner and chasing the butterf ies from f ower to f ower. She woke up refreshed from a deep slumber in a very happy frame of mind and wrote a long letter to her childhood friend Bipasha:

–Syracuse

My Dearest Friend,

Life has treated me very cruelly! I have been dumped in a new country and am feeling lonely, sinking lower and lower in a fathomless abyss and slowly dying literally speaking. I don't know how long I would survive. May be, this is my last letter to you.

Yes! You were right in your assessment of Prem, the scoundrel but you had under-estimated that crook, he turned out to be a much greater rouge. He told me three days back that he is already married and his American wife and kid live in New York. Yesterday he has left this place with all his baggage and most probably he won't return. In one way I am happy that he has gone out of my life though I feel very unclean and wretched to have shared the same bed with him for so many days.

That leaves me as a deserted woman dumped by the so-called husband, stranded in a new country with no money, no friends and no hope. I am paralyzed by depression, despondency and loneliness. It seems I have only two choices – either to return to India and lead a shameful life or to commit suicide to end all this nightmare once and for all. But if I can murder that man before dying, I will have no regrets.

How I wish, I was with you now!

–Kamlesh

PS: Pl don't tell anything to my parents, they are the ones who have ruined my life in the f rst place.

-20-

After going back to Montreal Sushovan did not join Alembic, sent them a regret letter and started applying for post-doctoral fellowships to various universities and institutes. In about a month he started getting offers. He got an offer from Stevens Institute of Technology in Hoboken, New Jersey, USA and joined there. In a few more months, Nilanjana f nished her M.A. During summer vacations Santanu and his family were going to Kolkata and Indrani persuaded Lopamudra also to be there during that time so that she could meet her parents and talk about the marriage of Sushovan with Nilanjana and she agreed. The parents of Lopa's husband were getting old and wanted to see their grandchildren. Her in-laws were living with their elder son and Lopa was to stay with them.

In Kolkata Indrani and her family went to see Lopamudra and in the evening Lopa and Nilanjana along with her brother and sister-in-law came to meet Indrani's parents. Indrani introduced them to her parents. Indrani's mother was very happy to see Nilanjana, asked her to come and sit beside her and told her "because of you Sushovan has decided to come back to India and all of us are thankful to you for that."

It was decided that Sushovan would come for two weeks during July to get married in Delhi, thereafter would come to Kolkata to meet the elders and would thereafter directly go back to US along with his wife from there.

***

Harish suddenly returned to Delhi from Solan in October while he was in his f nal year. Aroras were very happy to see him and presumed that he had come during Dushera vacations. However when Harish did not show any inclination to go back even after three weeks or so, they started getting worried. Harish did not go out to meet his friends, always used to remain gloomy and spent most of his times upstairs in his room. Poonam felt that his son had changed very much due to hostel life. He also always wanted more pocket money and Poonam wondered what did he do with the money as he seldom went out. After about a month of his stay, a court summons suddenly came in his name, asking him to appear in the court at Shimla on next Monday.

The letter surprised and shocked his father and he summoned his son. At f rst, Harish maintained a stoic silence but on persistent questioning, broke down and narrated his side of the story- "I along with three of my friends from the hostel had gone to see the night show of a movie on one night. The hostel gates used to be closed at nine, every night. On our return while we were silently scaling the gates for entering into the hostel, the night watchman suddenly saw us, shouted and came running. He caught one of my friends and a scuff e followed. The watchman fell at some point and was injured. The other watchman reached the spot on hearing the noise and found his colleague bleeding profusely and reported the warden. The night watchman told the names of all four of us and in fear, all of us decided to run away from the hostel." He looked at his father.

The injured night watchman had to be hospitalized and his family had lodged on FIR against all the four boys. It had become a Police case. The situation was very grave. Arora felt the court summon indicated there was something more to it. He decided to f rst go to Solan along with his son, meet the hostel warden, as well as the principal of the college, hear the whole story and then proceed to Shimla to face the court. After reaching Solan, he met the Warden of the hostel f rst.

The warden told him that Harish had fallen in bad company. They had been caught once while taking drugs in their hostel room and had been given stern warning. He further said, "The principal had written a strong letter to you asking for a reply and since you had promised on behalf of your son that such incident won't be repeated, so Harish was spared."

Arora was surprised "I did not get any such letter and had neither sent any reply" and looked sternly to his son. The warden said "in that case, he must have intercepted your letter at some point and had himself sent a reply forging your signature."

On seeing the court summon the warden explained: "this is a very grave situation and your son has to bear the consequences of his action."

Arora was puzzled "what action". The warden was surprised "you don't know? The night watchman died in the hospital on the third day, but before that, on the second day, he had given a statement to the police that when he had caught the boys at night scaling the gates, they were intoxicated and Harish had hit him from behind with an iron rod, causing a big fracture in the skull. This fact was later corroborated by the other night watchman and also by his three friends during interrogation by the Police."

Arora asked, "what happened to his other friends?"

"All of them were from Himachal Pradesh, they were nabbed and brought here by Police. The main murder charge has been slapped on Harish while other accomplices present on the crime scene have been charged with lesser offences. They have given a written statement to the Police about what had transpired. All the four have thereafter been rusticated from the college."

Arora went from there to the Principal who corroborated what the warden had said. On asking for some leniency regarding the punishment he sternly refused. "These boys were casting evil inf uences on other students and have been charged with serious crimes like using drugs and being involved in the murder. No, sorry! No mercy could be shown to them. They are all grown up and will have to face the consequences for their action."

Arora went to Shimla along with his son and had to engage a lawyer to defend his son in the criminal case. He found a lawyer Negi, who was incidentally from Solan. During the court proceeding, the Judge listened to the case being made by the public prosecutor and gave a date for the next month to hear the plea of the lawyer from the defendant's side.

Arora was very concerned and asked Negi about the outcome of the case. Negi was an experienced lawyer and said "the case will drag on for quite some time and being a murder accused, Harish may face life imprisonment in the worst scenario, though I will try my best to reduce the charges."

Arora asked, "Is there any chance for that?"

"See! All the evidence are against him but if the night watchman's family does not press the charges further then there may be found some way to reach an out of the court settlement. You may try to talk to the family and give them suff cient incentives to withdraw the case. They are poor people and I hope you understand what I mean?"

Arora nodded "yes I do", being a businessman he was well aware of the power of money in such cases.

Arora asked, "and if they don't agree?"

Negi was serious, pondered for a while and said "the only way then would be to stretch the case longer, to buy time and think for something. But mind you the public prosecutor will not allow it."

Arora was worried "but then how could he buy more time?"

Negi was hesitant "though as a lawyer I should not tell this perhaps it could be arranged if your son goes into some kind of hiding and we will say that he is ill or something like that and in the meantime I will request for new dates and hope for the best."

Arora nodded but could see that it would cost him a fortune to get out of this nasty situation. He was very angry with his son and scolded him right and left but, he felt that if his son is not pulled out of this situation, his whole life would be ruined and as a father he could not accept this.

He went back to Solan, went alone to the watchman's ramshackle cottage on the periphery of the town and met the widow. She was about thirty-f ve, sitting in her makeshift sort of shop, displaying some vegetables, grocery items and cheap stationery and was assisted by her elder son, may be ten years old while the younger son about six years or so old, was playing in front of the shop. Arora did not disclose his identity and she mistook him as someone from amongst her husband's employers, she asked him "how much more time it would take to get his dues from the college?"

He gave her some vague answer and asked about her source of livelihood after expressing profound grief over the death of her husband. She started crying "my both the sons were in school but as I could not pay the fees, their names have been struck".

He asked, "how much are the fees?" "Sixty rupees"

Arora took out his wallet and gave her a f ve hundred rupee note and said: "please pay their fees for the whole year and see that their study is not disrupted."

She took the note and thanked him profusely, then said "as a side business I ran this shop but now I do not have any money to buy the provisions. I don't know how I will feed them?"

He gave her three more f ve hundred rupee notes and asked her "with part of this money you replenish your shop and use the rest of the money to run your household. In the meantime, I would try to expedite the process to clear your dues soon."

She was overwhelmed with this generosity of his employers and asked her two sons to touch the feet of the masterji.

Arora asked her "Is it your cottage?" She replied proudly "yes, two years back my husband had bought this land and we had planned to renovate this cottage by next year. Now I don't know how I would be able to do it" and again started crying.

Arora consoled her "Don't worry, pray to God and he would show you some way." He gave them another f ve hundred rupee note to buy the winter clothing's for the whole family and said "whatever happened has already happened. Your sons are your insurance for the future and see that they f nish their school education" and came away. He went to his hotel and along with Harish returned to Delhi.

-21-

The whole managing committee of Himadri apartment was shocked and protested loudly against the unethical and blatant money power demonstration by one of its residents Indra Jeet Parasher who was a moneyed man of around sixty-f ve years of age and very sweet-tongued. Parashar owned a guest house in Panchsheel Park which had lately achieved some degree of notoriety. It was being whispered by some people that its clientele had the dubious distinction of entertaining call girls there and other shady businesses.

Parasher lived in a ground f oor three bedroom f at, had two full-time servants and already had a brush with RWA for having encroached the entire front side portion of his f at by putting rows of f ower pots all around the entire common area, as a result, nobody could pass from the area. His neighbours had complained to the President and only two weeks back, all the members of the RWA led by President Juneja had come there along with the society gardener to throw away all the pots and clear the encroachment of the common space. At that time Parashar's family had gone somewhere. After he returned, his servants complained to him and there was a big ruckus with him on one side and the entire M.C. on the other side backed by residents of his block.

His son Sunil lived in Nauroji Nagar and used to come frequently to meet his parents along with his wife and a sixteen-year-old son Anil, studying in high school and a daughter three or four years younger. Last evening while Sunil was on a visit there, the family went inside to meet the parents but Anil took from his father the key of the Maruti-800 car and was having a good driving practice by going round and round, exiting by the gate No. 2 to the main road and re-entering through the gate No. 1, thus covering a distance of about four hundred meters in each round. The stretch of the road from gate No. 1 had become narrow due to the parking of cars and he was coming in high speed. The press wallah's four-year-old daughter was crossing the road at that instant, Anil could not control his speed, hit her head on and she was thrown more than ten feet away coming down with a big thud and her body becoming still. She was dead on the spot, killed instantly. The watchman from the gate saw it, as well as some residents who happened to be passing from there. It had already become dark and the street lights were on. The watchman came running and also the residents. Within f ve minutes there was a crowd. Anil, in the meantime, had sped away from the scene, stopped his car in front of his grand father's house, quietly went inside and sat with his parents.

There was a big commotion. The press- wallah, his wife and his sons came running, his wife crying loudly carrying the dead daughter in her arms and all of them along with, watchman and some residents came to Parashar's house, they were all very agitated and a resident called Mr. Parashar to come out. As he and Sunil came out, the watchman complained "your grandson Anil was driving the Maruti car, has hit and killed Presswallah's daughter" and showed the wailing wife with the dead daughter in her arms.

At f rst, they did not believe him but the angry crowd joined him and showed the car's front portion where a torn piece of cloth with some f esh and fresh blood was still clinging to the metal. The Presswallah's wife was crying hysterically and cursing the whole family for killing her daughter.

By now the other watchman had informed the security-in-charge, Kaul and he along with Juneja, Secretary Bhatia and some more residents also reached there. Juneja had already informed the police and asked the Presswalah to lodge an FIR as it was a hit and run case causing death. The Presswallah was illiterate, so Kaul and Bhatia wrote the FIR on his behalf and together they took him to the Police Station in Chittranjan Park, lodged the FIR, received a copy, duly signed by Police and returned.

While they were in the police station, Parashar had sweet-talked to the wife of Presswalah, who was still wailing with her dead child in her laps, to arrange for the last rites of the body in the night itself and by about ten at night, after the Presswalah returned from the police station, took the entire family in their cars to the burning ghat, arranged for the pyre etc. at his expenses and fed also the entire family with food cooked at his home. The Presswallah and his wife were very impressed with the generosity of Parashar and thus had agreed that there was no point in keeping the body for the next morning.

Next morning Juneja found the Presswallah was no more interested in slapping charges on the culprit. Anil had not only killed the child with rash driving but also, he was underage and had no driving licence. Police had said that it was an added offence and the RWA felt that it was the right moment to nail Parashar.

After about a week the residents found that Parashar had taken the Presswallah to the bank to make a Fixed deposit of ₹5000/- made in the name of his other daughter telling that this amount was for her marriage in ten years or so by which time the money would grow to around ₹15000/- or more. Also, he offered several thousand rupees to the family as cash compensation and bought them a new big table instead of his small ramshackle table made of packing boxes and a heavy new press for his business. The entire family had never seen so much money in their entire life and were proud to have such a decent and comfortable arrangement for their business. The Press wallah and his wife were quite satisf ed with what Parashar had done for them and agreed that they would not be able to get back their daughter by pursuing the case and so gave it in writing that they were voluntarily and of their free will were withdrawing the case against the accused.

In the meantime Parashar arranged to get a fake birth certif cate made for his grandson proving that he was over eighteen years of age and also got a driving licence made in his name from somewhere with effect from a back date which proved Anil was in possession of a valid driving license at the time of accident, thus exonerating him from the other crime also. It was well known that in Delhi you can get made any number of such licenses with proper payment to the touts and a very large number of drivers freely driving on Delhi roads with such fake licenses, making the roads so unsafe especially for the pedestrians. Police were also quite aware of this practice. Parashar paid a good sum to the police also, they found everything in order and ultimately the case was hushed up. The only damage was that the driving license of Anil was cancelled for two years and he was f ned ₹2000/- with a stern warning not to drive a car for next two years or face a jail sentence. The residents were very sore about the way the Parashar family deftly managed to slip away from the hands of law because of his blatant money power.

***

Lately, Nandini was feeling some discomfort in her throat and though it was nothing much to worry about. But it was persisting; her voice was becoming hoarse and also she was unable to speak loudly. She thought it could be due to strain on her vocal cord due to singing and to give herself some rest, she stopped taking fresh students since last few months thus reducing her singing hours. This helped her in devoting more time to Reema and the grandson and everybody was happy. She felt if her throat condition still did not improve she would see some specialist after Reema went away as there was no hurry.

Reema's second son was delivered normally in Sukhda hospital in G.K.-I. The Agrawals, as well as her in-laws, were also very happy, with the news and Agrawal distributed sweets among the neighbours. His son-in-law captain Amreesh came on a short leave of a week after three months and he took her to his parents at Dehradun. He was expecting a promotion after a few months with transfer to a family area and was planning to take his family with him thereafter. Till that time Reema was to live with her in-laws. Agrawal was now devoting much of his time in co-operative stores as stores-in-charge and the stores were running very successfully. It had started stocking some vegetables, fruits and gift items also on popular demand and it had raised the sales to a higher level.

-22-

Dr. Gautam Tripathi, after completing two years as P.D.F. in Stevens Institute of technology at New Jersey, was offered the Post of Asst. Professor in the faculty on the strength of his brilliant academic career and more than ten research publications, most of them in reputed American journals. He accepted the job and f nally settled in an academic career. He was in the same department where Sushovan was working and they as well as their wives became good friends. Gautam's mother informed him that Saurav's marriage had been settled with one Shreya the only daughter of one Dr. Mishra who was Asst. Director in Central Drug Research Institute, Lucknow. Shreya was a school teacher and was also a very good singer, an artist of All India Radio, Lucknow and that they would be informed as and when the marriage dates were f nalized.

Dr. Saurav by now had completed his M.S. and was now a Senior Resident in the department of surgery. He had bought a motorcycle for commuting to medical college and was regularly assisting his professors in the operation theatre (O.T.) and Out Patient's Deptt. (OPD) and once or twice a week had a roster of twenty-four-hour duty. In the night shifts he was required to look after the critical cases, some of them in I.C.Us (Intensive Care Units). He found that the attitude of some of the doctors and mainly the nurses, was very practical bordering almost to callousness, towards the patients. They looked at the patients more as an object rather than a living being. Sometimes while handing over the charge, they will very casually remark – bed no. 5 would not survive another day or during night shifts if he found that the duty nurses were sleeping in the off ce and if he woke them up and reminded them" the patients of bed no. 8 and 14 require special attention. Why don't you administer the medicine immediately as their B.P. has already gone down to sixty."

They would reply "Sir, those two patients are gone cases anyway. Bed No. 14 is already eighty years old and even her family members don't seem to care". He would remind "even then, as doctors we should do our best" and she would reply philosophically "we are doing our best but ultimately it is in His hands" and look upwards. Probably the routine job of looking after the patients year after year and realizing the inevitability of death had toughened them to a point where the patient for them had become only a number."

But there were good sides also. A patient in ICU had died in the evening but his senior instructed him "Don't declare him dead right now. There is a marriage in his family tonight, let us wait till the ceremony is over."

"But madam, rigour Mortis is already setting in."

"I know, just keep your attempts to revive him continue for some more time."

Dr. Saurav was still hesitant "the body has to be shifted to the mortuary and if it is not shifted within an hour or so, the staff who are on general duty, would leave and then it could be shifted only tomorrow morning. More important another patient in bed No. 23 is becoming critical and has to be shifted to ICU soon in his place."

"O.K. I would arrange the patient to be shifted to another ICU" and off she went.

***

Bipasha had received the letter from Kamlesh and was very perturbed. For a day or two she kept brooding about the misery of her best friend and then wrote her a reply.:

New Delhi

Dear Kamlesh

Was very disturbed by your letter but I am thankful that you have trusted and have shared your feelings with me. I fully understand your position and your state of mind but will warn you that being emotional you will not be able to solve your problems. Please don't do anything in haste and listen to me, no self-pity either.

When we were in our middle school, do you remember that we used to play a game of staring into each other's eyes and whosoever blinked f rst was the loser? In the whole class, you used to be the winner and we all used to admire you for your will power. You are still the same person, I would wish that you stare into the face of the misfortune with the same boldness and not be cowed down by them. I would strongly advise you not to contemplate coming back to India in this condition as a loser at this stage. You are well aware of what will be your future in our country. Our society, as it is, will indirectly or directly hold you guilty for this misfortune, you would not be considered of any value in the marriage market and would be pitied upon.

My suggestion is that you stay on in that country. Nobody knows you there and even if they know that society is much more liberal as far as the marriage is concerned. Women enjoy much more freedom there to pursue their interests and there is much less gender discrimination. Remember that you are in USA, which is the land of opportunities! I am sure if you only try, you would get more opportunities there to stand on your own legs i.e. I mean to manage life without any support from others.

You were always brighter than me as a student. If I have been able to pursue my post-graduation and aspire to do my Ph.D, I am sure you also can still do it. I understand that there is a university in Syracuse and my advice is, get out of your shell, go to the university and try it to get into the graduate studies programme. You have already descended to the bottom of the pit, you can not go any further down. So please muster all your courage and start climbing up. You may call it my audacity of hope but I have the f rm belief that you have the steel in you to rise again. Yes! You can do it! I am praying to God with all my heart to give you strength. Our greatest glory lies not in falling, but rising each time we fall! And your time starts right now!!

–Yours Bip

Bipasha could not, however, bear to keep the misery of Kamlesh to herself and after a few days told her mother. Indrani got very much concerned and told Santanu after he came back from the off ce. He immediately called Bipasha, saw the letter and told Indrani to immediately inform the Aroras. So Indrani along with Bipasha went to

Neelachal Apt on the same evening and showed the letter to Poonam. Arora became very angry to learn that Prem had turned out to be a such a scoundrel but Poonam started crying uttering "Wahe Guru! Why are you punishing my daughter for no fault of hers? Our son is already in the deep trouble and as if that is not enough, now you have put our daughter in a worse state" and she went on wailing "why did she not tell us earlier? And clung to Bipasha who also joined her in crying but then straightened up "Uncle! As a f rst step, please send her some money." This brought everybody to their senses and Poonam asked her husband to immediately book a call to her and he complied. Bipasha and Indrani returned to their f at.

<h1 style="text-align:center">-23-</h1>

Dr. Saurav Tripathi had retained a room in the hostel especially for taking some rest after the night shifts and for freshening up purposes after twenty-four-hour duties. He was very tired that morning after f nishing a twenty-four-hour duty during which two emergency operations also had been performed. While he was going to his room in the hostel, Dr. Tandon who was a Senior Resident in anaesthesia called him and handed him an envelope which was lying in his department. Dr.Saurav kept it in his coat pocket, opened his room, threw away the coat on the chair and hit the bed right away.

After a few hours of sleep, he felt fresh, ordered his lunch and went to the toilet. After the lunch, while he was having the dessert, he looked around the room and saw one envelope lying on the f oor below the chair and remembered Dr. Tandon having given him the envelopes. He picked it up. The address was:

Dr. Saurav Tripathi

M.S.

Medical College, Kanpur

He looked at the postmark and understood why the letter had taken more than a week to reach him, leisurely he opened the letter and straightened up instantly on going through it:

Dr. Tripathi,

Lucknow

Perhaps you are aware that our parents have f xed our marriage, only the dates remain to be f nalized. I am in a very desperate situation and am urgently in need of your help. I am writing this letter in strict conf dence, with the hope that you would keep it only to yourself. My situation cannot be explained in a letter and so I would request if you could meet me alone and soon, sometime, at Lucknow. If yes, suggest a date and time at the following address:

Shreya Mishra

Teacher; Jubille Girl's School,

Lucknow

Eagerly looking forward to meeting you.

–Regards,

Shreya

Saurav read the letter several times and his f rst reaction was that his father must have asked for dowry, even though he had strictly expressed his feelings against it. After two days he sent her a short reply:

Kanpur

Miss Shreya Mishra

Received your letter though I must frankly admit that I am unable to guess as to how I would be able to help you. Hope face to face discussion between us would be more useful. I propose let us have lunch together on coming Saturday at Royal Café in Hazratgunj, say at one P.M. If it suits you please convey your acceptance over my mobile and the number is 98....

Rest on seeing you.

–Saurav

Shreya accepted the invitation and informed him over telephone accordingly. On Saturday Saurav came to Lucknow on his bike, they met at the front door of Royal Café at the scheduled time, he noted that besides being beautiful she was having a lovely f gure also and went inside, ushered to a corner table and sat down. As he was slightly dishevelled after more than one hour's driving, he went to the toilet for freshening up. He looked much refreshed on coming back, asked her to order lunch as per her preference and she did.

Both kept sitting silently for some time and then Dr. Saurav took the initiative "I understand that you are in a tight spot so let us begin straightway without any formal weather report or something" and smiled. This helped in opening up Shreya who was still hesitant and began "I don't know how to tell you but I guess I have to be honest with you."

Saurav nodded "I would very much appreciate that way. You can trust me and be frank."

"Well! in that case, let me start from the beginning. During my school years, we used to live in Aminabad locality where we had a neighbour whose son Mureed Siddiqui was my childhood friend. We both were good singers, we were called to sing at the neighbour's get-togethers and functions of the locality. By the time we grew up, we started to go together to sing on stage in bigger functions in other localities of Lucknow both solo and in duets. Our songs clicked, we were in demand and we started performing in front of large audiences and also on All India Radio, Lucknow." She paused for a while. Dr. Saurav commented, "under more favourable circumstances I also would have loved to hear you singing but anyway, please continue".

"We did not even realize when or how this togetherness changed into a mutual attraction for each other, but it did".

Dr. Saurav asked, "So much was happening and your family did not notice?"

She said, "No, they didn't know because, after my high school, we moved over to our new house in Mahanagar where you and your parents had come to see me."

He asked, "yes, I remember".

"However, we continued to meet each other, ostensibly in connection with our musical engagements, but even otherwise. After MA, B.Ed I became a teacher in Jubilee and he became a lecturer in D.A.V. College and we started to dream of a life together.

In the meantime, the waiter brought the lunch order and they started eating. About midway to the lunch, Dr. Saurav resumed "I can see your point but I don't understand how do I come into the picture?"

"See, my parents will not allow me to break the engagement and will make it a prestige issue but the more important thing being that they will never accept my marrying a Muslim boy though his parents will not object very much, as he says".

He interrupted "but still it is not clear as to how I would be able to help you."

She looked straight into his eyes "Suppose you refuse to marry me." He understood "but that would only temporarily solve the problem even if we assume that my parents at this stage will agree to my refusal, besides that your parents would look for other matches for you and let me tell you that other young men also will f nd it very hard to refuse you."

She blushed "we also have the same dilemma but at least it would buy us a little more time and so he also asked me to solicit your advice".

Dr. Saurav remained silent for a while and then smiled "can you see the black humour in what you are asking? You want me to be a co-conspirator with you in breaking my own marriage" he looked at her.

"Whatever way you may look at it but the outcome remains the same that it would give us some more time to f nd a way".

He nodded "I get your point. Just give me some time to think over. However, let me confess that I am getting very inquisitive to see that lucky chap of yours- Mureed who has won the heart of my would-be bride. Why don't you call him here right away to meet us?" and he gave his mobile to her to contact him.

The waiter was clearing the table and Dr. Saurav ordered two coffee. She telephoned Mureed, fortunately, his classes were over and he was about to leave and promised to be there inside half an hour.

Saurav asked her "do you think you would be happy with him?"

"Yes, we know each other since childhood, know each other's families also and understand each other well."

Dr. Saurav asked her bluntly "let me ask you a personal question, which you are free if you don't want to reply." She said "OK".

"I am very curious to know whether you already have had a physical relationship?" She looked away and replied, "only twice but after that, we have vowed to wait till marriage." He was very impressed with her frankness and asked her "How would your parents like your marrying a Muslim boy?"

"They would be very much against it. Ours is a very conservative Brahmin family."

"But since you have already decided to go for it, I guess you have to tell your parents sooner or later?"

Shreya looked up "They would raise hell, would create a scene and start emotionally blackmailing me and all that. So I have decided to tell them after the marriage only."

"Then what prevents you from getting married?"

"Mureed is scared".

"Why?" Dr. Saurav asked, "Because Vishwa Hindu Parishad which is very strong here, had recently politicized this issue as forced conversion of Hindu girls into Muslims and made it a big political browny point, including beating and harassing the boy including his family and community."

He asked, "you don't mind being a Muslim?"

Shreya replied "See Lucknow has a Muslim culture since long. In Aminabad where we lived earlier, we had many Muslim neighbours and we had very cordial relations with them. Muslims are also people just like us, only their religion is different. I consider religion is a matter of personal belief and Mureed also believes likewise. Moreover, we plan to live separately from our families after marriage, so we believe this issue of the cultural difference will not remain very important." Saurav asked, "Then why don't you marry and f nish this 'trishanku' position, I mean hanging in between?"

"See! He is ready but I have put a rider. I have asked him to appear for All India competitions and get some good job like in a Bank, L.I.C., Railways or U.P.S.C. etc. For the last year or so, he is trying. He has appeared in several examinations and is still trying and it is, in fact, a matter of time. I have a hunch he will get something sooner or later and then we will start a new life. In short, we need some more time" she looked at him.

"and if he fails to get one?"

She said "No, no, I have faith in his abilities, he is intelligent. He is trying sincerely and eventually, he will succeed."

Just then Mureed made his appearance. He was a lanky, fair-complexioned young man with medium height and sharp features. Shreya introduced him and Mureed while shaking hands smiled " I was scared that you would reject the idea outright but she seems quite relaxed, so it seems the talks are progressing and I still have some hope. I had asked Shreya to tell you honestly about our relationship and seek your advice, so let me think that by now you know our case?"

Dr. Saurav asked the waiter to bring tea and some snacks for three people. By this time the dining hall had become almost empty and the evening rush had not yet started. He turned to Mureed and admitted. "She has done a remarkable job and let me congratulate you Mr. Siddiqui………"

"No, Mureed would be f ne". "Well, Mureed, you are a lucky chap and though I am a little disappointed that you have spoiled my chances to marry this beautiful lady since you have already won her heart, she is yours by all means." Dr. Saurav said.

Both of them seemed very relieved and jointly said "thanks very much" Saurav protested "let there be no thank you between friends and you can consider me a friend".

Mureed stood up, clasped his hands and said from his innermost heart "there cannot be a better demonstration of friendship and you don't know how light-hearted I am feeling right now after tension-f lled last more than a month "and he looked at Shreya, who looked at Dr. Saurav "now, how do you advise us to Proceed?" Saurav thought for a while and then said "I have an idea. I would ask my parents to f nalise the date at least three months later, stating about my some immediate commitments in the hospital "and looked at Shreya" will that suit you?" and both of them jointly said" perfectly."

Then he looked at Mureed and asked him.

"Are you fully committed to marrying her within three months? Because if, after that time, I hear that you have still not married her, I may lose my patience and give a green signal to my parents. After all, such a beautiful lady cannot be asked to keep waiting indef nitely!" he Shrugged. Mureed felt very relieved "Dr. Tripathi…." Saurav interrupted "Saurav will be f ne". "Well! Saurav, I promise to marry her within three months" and he clasped Saurav's hands and further added, "not only that we would post you of the developments also in the meantime."

Dr. Saurav cleared the bills, got up for he had a night duty but before leaving he, as an after thought added "I feel, you should avoid controversies of religious marriage and go for a registered marriage. You both are adults and self-supporting, just go to the marriage registrar's off ce, submit an application and get quietly married after a month or so, instead of postponing it any further."

Both of them liked the idea and agreed that it would be the best course of action. Dr. Saurav added, "I will be glad to sign as a witness if you f nd it appropriate."

Mureed had made up his mind "Next week we would apply to the Registrar's off ce and yes, you would be the f rst witness from my side."

Shreya immediately protested "How can you say that. He will be a witness from my side and that is f nal. You f nd out somebody else" and they parted happily.

Next day, after night duty, when Dr. Saurav reached home, his mother came to him "Mishras are pressing for a date by next month or so. We also feel that we should not linger any further. What do you say?

He replied "ma, this happens to be the worst time for me. Presently I have tremendous work pressure as two of my colleagues are going on leave. Some vacancies are to be f lled up in three months or so and by that time my colleagues also would come back from leave and I would be able to relax. Why don't you f nalise the date after three months?"

His mother said, "No, no, it would mean after 15th December, but there is no marriage date for next month and that means, would be only after 15th January, which means it would be delayed by four months". But Saurav was f rm "then make it after 15th January only" and went away leaving his mother grumbling.

-24-

Manish f nished his masters in computer graphics from the University of Philadelphia, got a job in the Wall Street and moved to New York. For a few months, he rented a one-bedroom f at in the cheaper Lower Manhattan side and used to return to Philadelphia to his sister during the weekends. But in about six months, he bought a new Cortina car, felt he was well settled in the job which he liked, rented a two-bedroom accommodation on the second f oor of a house in a middle-class locality in 106th Street on the Fifth Avenue in upper Manhattan. It was a residential area with both whites and blacks living and the good thing was that they lived in harmony, both the communities had free mixing and there was no undercurrent of any communal tension.

He used to drive in the evenings on his northward journey back home, up to Central Park West, passing the Museum of Natural History, crossing the 86th Street until he reached 106th street and then turn left. A little further, on the right side was a small playground f lled with neighbourhood children playing, then a basketball court and cruising further, to the curb in front of the renovated brownstone house number 120 where he was a tenant on the second f oor. He did his light housekeeping and every fortnight or so he was driving to Philadelphia during the weekends to his sister. In between, he once went to India also, on leave. His father was getting old nearing seventy, his brother Anupam had passed B.Com but did not study any further and was presently mostly sitting at their crockery shop while Pasricha went only for an hour or two during the afternoons. Manish met his old friends but the bond of friendship was gone. Bipasha was now in M.Sc Final year and Partho in his second year at the Roorkee IIT. He tried to meet Priyanka but learnt that she had f nished her engineering and was working at Lucknow as her family had shifted there. Agrawal auntie had stopped taking music classes.

After Reema left, Nandini had gone to an E.N.T specialist in East of Kailash, who felt it could be the Singer's nodule, which often aff icts professional singers. He prescribed a heavy dose of antibiotics, advised her to stop giving music lessons immediately and asked her to come after a month. The treatment continued for two more months, but there were no discernible signs of improvement. Also, Nandini felt a great weakness and loss of appetite due to the continued intake of antibiotics. The specialist then advised Agrawal to take a second opinion and he suggested one Dr. Gaur in Sukhda hospital as the problem did not seem to respond to antibiotics. Dr. Gaur examined her, continued the line of treatment but changed the drug. However, as Nandini was feeling a sense of nausea, Agrawal decided to give a gap of one month to allow her to recover and then started the new drug. When she did not respond to even that, Dr. Gaur advised Agrawal to go to All India Institute of Medical Sciences (AIIMS). Again two more months elapsed but when Nandini started having occasional fever also, Agrawal ultimately took her to AIIMS. As usual, AIIMS was very crowded, they had to stand in long queues, but the doctors examined her thoroughly, asked her to come again and advised a series of pathological tests. After a fortnight or so, on the conclusion of all tests, they prescribed some medicines and asked her to come again after a month. On seeing no improvement even after that, they advised a biopsy to be done in their cancer wing. After going there she was given a date and asked her to come prepared to be admitted to their ward for a day.

***

Prem did not return from New York. Kamlesh was in a state of deep depression and was a total recluse, making minimum contacts with the outside world. She was also running out of her money and did not know what to do once the lease of the house expired and then she received Bipasha's letter. She read and reread it many times and slowly some ray of hope started coming back. Yes! Bip had shown a way out that was worth trying. The letter sort of rejuvenated her, acting as a tonic. She started thinking of the future course of action, her strength coming back. The life could not be worse than her present position she reasoned, if she had to get out of this mess, she had to help herself, nobody would come to her rescue. She went out, withdrew some money from her account, bought some provisions, tidied her house and herself and decided to go to face the world.

It was morning in USA, Kamlesh was having her breakfast and was getting ready to go to the University. Suddenly the telephone bell rang, she was surprised as to who could this be for she never received any telephone calls. She reluctantly lifted the receiver. She recognized the voice of her mother. The dam of all her pent up agony of the previous days burst and tears started f owing out of eyes uncontrollably. Both mother and daughter cried loudly over the phone for just few minutes and Poonam told her "talk to your father f rst" and gave the receiver to Arora.

Arora took the phone and said "Beti! please pardon your father for his indiscretion. Just forget about Prem, and don't take any step in a hurry. You are in a foreign country and all alone in a desperate situation but remember that your father is still alive. We will see what best could be done. We are happy that you have conf ded in Bipasha and told her. Now f rst thing f rst. Please tell me your account number and I will send you some money for your survival." She brought her passbook and gave him the details. This done, he said "We feel that you return as soon as you are ready. I will send more money for your ticket etc. on hearing from you and now you talk to your mother "he gave the phone to Poonam.

After getting the phone call from home, the zest for life started returning, her monetary situation was also going to ease soon and the worry on this account also being over, she went to the university.

○○○

<h1 style="text-align:center">-25-</h1>

Shreya called back after a week, while Dr. Saurav was making around in the ward. He came out and took the call "Thank you for coming to Lucknow and meeting us. Mureed is very impressed with you. We want to meet you again.... He protested "It looks like I am getting neck-deep in your conspiracy."

Shreya giggled "that is for certain, last night I overheard my parents discussing the marriage date." "what?"

"that the boy wants another three months. Mrs. Tripathi informed from Kanpur a few days back that at present he has some work commitments and would not be able to get any leave"

Saurav was relieved "thank God, the plea has worked."

Shreya was still not f nished "Now listen to the next part – my mother feels that you may be involved with some colleague of yours and may be bidding for your time to say no to us."

He immediately protested "that is grossly unfair! For all my sacrif ces I am now being branded as a villain"

Shreya agreed "I feel sorry for you. You know, earlier both Mureed and me had a notion that you must be a very serious person, not believing in the nonsenses like love and all that, vehemently protecting your family honour etc. Let me frankly admit I f nd you a very amiable, down to earth and sensible person........."

He brightened up "it is not too late even now for you to change your decision. Alas! Mureed came so much earlier in your life that I had no chance to compete to show you my many other brighter sides........."

She interrupted him "Oh! I forgot to tell you the main thing. We have applied in marriage registrar's off ce and would be called after one month. You will be my prime witness....."

"Who would be the other one?"

"My one colleague who knows about our affair".

Saurav could not resist some f irting "Is she as beautiful as you?"

"Why?"

"No, nothing! I was just taking my chances".

Shreya laughed "She is, but unfortunately she is already married. Anyway, thank you once again for suggesting the registree marriage. I would inform you the date and your presence would be a must". She switched off the phone.

The conspirators met again, in hotel Gomti, after a fortnight and this time Mureed was hosting the lunch. Shreya informed Dr. Saurav the date when he had to be present in the Registrar's off ce and Mureed informed "several months back, I had appeared for a combined Bank's examination for the Probationary off cer's Post. I have cleared the written test and they have called me for an interview in State Bank of India, Kolkata, next month". Dr. Saurav shook hands with him "Well! all the best and congrats in advance"

"Thanks"

Saurav then looked at Shreya "would you announce your marriage now?" "Not immediately, presently we will maintain the status quo. But after he gets the job, we would go wherever it is, start living together and then would announce the marriage".

Dr. Saurav said "My best wishes in advance for your happy future" and then added. I have retained a room in the hostel of my medical college which I use only from time to time. I suggest in case if you do not have any other plans, why don't you spend your honeymoon there as my guests. Consider that as my marriage gift" he looked at them.

Both Shreya and Mureed looked at each other and said "we would let you know. At present we have not thought about anything regarding the honeymoon." Saurav concluded "fair enough! my invitation stands any way!!" and left.

Mureed and Shreya were married in the registrar's off ce on the scheduled date with Dr. Saurav as one of the witnesses. The newly married couple had decided in favour of honeymoon at Kanpur and so went along with Saurav, the married couple on one Bike and Saurav leading them on his bike. On the way Mureed told him the good news that his appointment letter for the probationary off cer's post had come with posting at SBI, Bara Bazar branch at Kolkata and Shreya had given notice to the school for resigning her job. Saurav arranged a small get together in the common room of his hostel in honour of the newly married couple and requested them to sing a few songs, and they obliged. The few songs stretched into a more than one hour programme with the common room getting jam-packed with eager listeners and their requests to hear more of their melodious voices. Both were very good singers and had a lot of promise for the future.

Fortunately, their marriage did not raise much religious controversy when news leaked out at Lucknow but it raised suff cient storm in the house of Saurav at Kanpur as well as at Lucknow. Dr. Mishra was furious with his daughter when she declared her marriage in the house. Both her parents were in a f t of rage for this ungrateful, impertinent and dishonourable act of their daughter to marry without their consent and knowledge and that too with a Muslim. Dr. Mishra announced very loudly "I feel so ashamed and don't know how I will convey this news to Dr. Tripathi, face them and be humiliated by them because of you "he pointed an accusing f nger to Shreya. Her mother was still not believing how their daughter, who is a teacher, could go for such a dishonourable act knowingly when her marriage was f xed with such a bright doctor boy from a very respectable family. She demanded to see the marriage certif cate and when they learnt that Dr. Saurav was one of the witnesses of her marriage, Dr. Mishra was surprised and demanded to know how Dr. Saurav came to know about it?

"I had told him".

Her mother was shocked by this admission "and he agreed to be your witness?"

Shreya nodded "yes".

Her parents looked at each other and felt very relieved. Dr. Mishra as if in a monologue exclaimed "I don't understand the young people of this generation. In my time this act could have led to some honour killings from both sides or at least life long hostility between the two families "and in a huff, he left the room. However, the parents, when they were alone, admitted that Shreya, by involving Saurav, had wisely blunted some of the accusations from Dr. Tripathi's side.

Both Jay Shankar Tripathi as well as Jaya strongly disapproved the part played by his son in this dishonourable secret marriage and thought it a very irresponsible act, to say the least. "He should have kept him totally out of the picture even if the girl had informed him", Dr. Tripathi was very angry "I was charged by Dr. Mishra that my son was an accomplice in this unholy and dishonourable act of his daughter". "Instead of reporting the matter in time so that this marriage could be prevented. Saurav connives with her and signs as a witness in the off ce of the marriage registrar." He fumed and admonished his son "you should have looked at the honour of your family at least."

Jaya also joined "that shrewd girl manipulated you by dragging you through sweet talking into this whole disreputable act. Even if you had been informed, at the least you should have stayed away from it and surely should have refused to sign at a witness. You can not afford to be so liberal in life as going against your interests. By involving you she has taken care of not only to minimize her parent's embarrassment in facing us but also in showing that her decision was not so dishonourable after all."

All the pleas of Saurav did not change the views of his parents. There was a rift between him and them and the earlier bonhomie was lost. That was the heavy price Dr. Saurav had to pay for being a party in breaking his marriage. Dr. Saurav new started feeling a void in his life. In retrospect, he felt that since Shreya had conf ded in him, a total stranger to her, he was honour bound in helping her even at the cost of breaking his marriage. Moreover, after knowing all about their intimate relationship, how could he have gone on to marry her against her wishes. His friends though appreciated his noble gesture of chivalry but felt that he should have been a bit more worldly-wise in saving his own and his family's interests. He started feeling very dissatisf ed with life, started applying for jobs abroad and after about three months and several telephonic interviews got a call from British Embassy in Delhi in connection with a job in a hospital at Cardiff and left for London in April. His ambition was to become a super-specialist in neurosurgery.

-26-

Bipasha had completed her M.Sc. and had appeared for the qualifying exams for Ph.D. also. Fortunately for her and unfortunately for her parents, she was awarded a Junior Research fellowship for joining the Ph.D. programme. This meant her parents had to stop looking for a match for her for at least three more years, to enable her to complete the Ph.D.

Nandini's biopsy had been carried out and the doctors diagnosed it as throat cancer. Agrawal was a very worried man, he had not told his wife about the diagnosis, but the worst part was, the doctors felt that the patient was very late in coming for the treatment and cancer seemed to have crossed over to the second stage. Nandini's fever started persisting for a longer time, she was, besides, losing weight and having diff culty in swallowing solid food, thus being given food in liquid or Slurry form. Doctors suggested a course of radiation treatment over eight weeks. She was given a mask to wear, for the administration of a strong dose of rays, which covered her entire head and face except for a small hole in the throat region from where the rays were to pass, to protect her from exposure to rays. The medicines were also very strong, it produced nausea, to itching sensation all over the body and also a general weakness. She had to be taken to the hospital every alternate day in the morning, coming back only in the evening. One combined effect of the ray and medicines was the complete hair loss from her scalp. By the time the treatment was more than halfway, she became bald and looked like a ghost of her former self.

Both her elder daughters came in turn and stayed for a month each, during the treatment but then they had to go back to their places. Reema then came from Dehradun, leaving behind her elder son with their in-laws. Amrish had been transferred to Jammu and was expecting to get family accommodation soon. After that, he was to come to Delhi, take Reema to Dehradun, stay there for a few days and then proceed to Jammu with his family from there.

On completion of the course of ray treatment Nandini's condition started improving slowly and in a fortnight or so she became almost normal. She had to take lots of fruits and she started taking Semi liquid diet with a result that her strength started coming back. Everybody was very happy and she started resuming her household duties also. At the end of one month, Amreesh came and Reema went away with him. Agrawal's had already employed a cook for the last two years or so and Reema instructed her mother not to strain herself very much with the kitchen work.

Indrani and Mrs. Baluja had come to see her in the afternoon and they were talking in her sitting room. Nandini asked Mrs. Baluja "you seem to have managed your life alone very well and seem to be physically quite f t also, what is the secret?"

Mrs. Baluja who was now nearing about seventy and slightly elder to Nandini said "at f rst I felt very helpless when Shobha took me to Pune along with her. While staying there, I realized that they had their own lives and I should not remain dependent on them as long as my body allows. You know, Mr. Baluja was a very independent man and we had planned to live independently all along. In Pune I used to see Shobha driving around freely, as a result, she was very independent as far as her mobility was concerned. She pressed me to learn driving whereas I was planning to sell off our car. During my stay at Pune, I decided to come back and face my life alone".

Nandini quipped "and as it turned out, it was a very good decision."

Mrs. Baluja agreed. "After coming back here, Garima stayed with me for a month. I joined the driving classes on her proddings".

She took me to banks for submitting my bills etc. and persuaded me to handle my f nancial matters, helped me in doing the necessary paper works so that I could independently handle the transactions as the owner and this gave me a new conf dence. After two months I got the driving licence but I did not have the conf dence to drive independently. Garima used to sit beside me initially, escorted me to the petrol pumps, car mechanic, in the Alkapuri and GK-II "M" Block markets, taught me to park the car properly and after three months I gained the necessary skill to drive alone in the locality. This free mobility gave me new conf dence.

Indrani got very enthused "I will also start taking driving lessons. Santanu had repeatedly asked me to learn driving, I had joined driving classes also but once, while reversing, I hit a wall and damaged the car considerably. That shattered my conf dence and I made no further attempts to hone the skill again" Mrs. Baluja laughed "Oh! These things would happen, they are part of the learning process."

Indrani said, "but Santanu was sitting beside me at that time and he scolded me right and left, just short of physically hitting me". Nandini smiled" my daughters tell me never to learn driving with your husband sitting beside you, they take sadistic pleasure in proving that you can never learn how to drive. By their constant guidance, they will drive you crazy and you won't be able to concentrate on driving."

Mrs. Baluja resumed. "After I learnt to drive around the locality, Garima took me to the outer Ring Road and main roads, initially I was very nervous, could not see the traff c signals or did not keep the car in the proper lanes, but she would immediately caution me and in another month or so I gained the conf dence to drive around freely and all these helped me in leading an independent life alone."

Nandini asked, "but how you cope up with the loneliness part of the life?" Mrs. Baluja replied "the secret is to keep yourself busy, see! f rst thing in the morning, I regularly go for at least half an hour or so of brisk walking, then sit for the yoga class there. In the park, you meet people, talk to them, feel connected and that keeps your spirits up. Then I come back, do the daily chore, f nish my cooking in the forenoon, read the paper, take nap in the afternoon, again go out in the evenings in the market or meet friends in the GK-II park. On Sundays, I go to the Gurdwara, help in community cooking for the langar, sweep the premises etc. Other widows also come there, we chit chat. Five of us friends, all widows frequently go for outings together, go for an annual trip to hill stations or other places. I give my services in our co-operative stores regularly for an hour or so, I have also joined a 'kirtan mandli', we sing bhajans in the houses of the locality on various occasions whenever people call us. My daughters tell me that I have become busier, living alone".

Your situation is very tough, but you seem to have made it look so easy going, I feel you are leading a very meaningful and active life. I wish every single woman should have your mental strength."

Nandini asked "you are physically f t, you are still capable of doing all your work by yourself, but after a few years when your body would refuse to go along, what will you do?

Mrs. Baluja had an answer for that also" the aunty of one of my friends lives in an old age home for ladies in Patel Nagar. She regularly goes there to meet her aunty, I have also gone with her many times. The inmates there are looked after well. It is a nice place but a bit expensive. My friend feels that when she would become older, f nding it diff cult to live alone, she will also go there. I also have lately started feeling the same way. I will give my f at on rent and with the income, I would be able to live there without being a burden on anyone". Nandini agreed and said " I am not a writer, had I been so, I would have surely written about your story. It is so inspiring."

Mrs. Baluja said "there is no point in cursing your fate and feel everything is over in life and thereby conf ne yourself into a shell. I have just gone out and met people to get over the loneliness problem, made myself socially useful by participating in the activities of the community, thereby keeping me busy thus trying to cope in a best possible way of living alone."

Nandini nodded and said "I also have three daughters, they all ask us to come and stay with them for a while......."

Indrani interrupted "but I have not seen you going to them often and even if you go, you come back only after a few days."

Nandini replied that is true, but there is a reason. My two elder daughters stay with their in-laws. Their house is big enough and they are quite keen that we should stay with them for a longer period but Mr. Agrawal does not feel very comfortable there and does not prolong our stay."

Indrani asked "why?". "because whatever you may say about the son and daughter being equal and all that, but the fact remains that the son is a son, the society approves the dependent old parents living with the son or the son living with the parents but there is still some stigma attached to the married daughter's parents living with her or the son-in-law living with the wife's parents. Thus the son's parents seem to have the f rst rights to stay with them when compared to the daughter's parents Mr. Agrawal feels that our status there is only as a visitor and so we are not expected to stay there long, at least as long as my daughter's in-laws are staying with them."

Mrs. Baluja agreed "My husband also did not want to go to my elder daughter Garima as she was staying with her in-laws in Ludhiana at that time."

Nandini continued "Mr. Agrawal feels more comfortable to stay in the daughter's house if their in-laws are not staying with them and that happens rarely as they go very seldom to their other son because they don't pull on well with the other son's wife." Mrs. Baluja asked "and what about Reema's place? She replied, "her in-laws stay with them permanently." Indrani was puzzled "so it means, son and daughter are not equals, after all, the son is a son and daughter is a daughter whatever we may say about equality."

Nandini said "why do you think that even the rich parents want a son more than a daughter.

Indrani protested "but it is not as per your choice"

Nandini continued "see, even in South Delhi which is supposed to be quite prosperous, female foeticide is much more rampant as a consequence of which the female population ratio is going down progressively. Anyway, you have both son and a daughter let them get married and then you will f nd out the difference."

Mrs. Baluja concurred "you can not think of living with your daughter, not at least, as long as their in-laws are living with them."

-27-

Sushovan joined as a post-doctoral fellow (PDF) in the Lab of Prof. Mitra in New Jersey. Stevens Institute of Technology was a very well known research centre and four PDFs were working with prof. Mitra, Sushovan included. This was in addition to seven graduate students working toward their Ph.D.s, Dr. Mitra was from Kolkata, was in this institute for the last f fteen years and had made a name for himself in the f eld of recombinant DNA and amino acid sequences in genes. He used to call his whole research group along with their wives for dinner twice a year. Sushovan and Nilanjana were attending the dinner party for the f rst time. Dr. Gautam Tripathi who had joined Dr. Mitra's group initially as a PDF and now was Asst. Professor in the dept. was also included in his group and had joined the party along with his wife Suman.

Sushovan introduced Nilanjana with his colleagues Dr. Prabir Majumdar from Kolkata and his wife Deepa, Dr. Tripathi and his wife Suman, and graduate students Anuradha Goswami from Mumbai, Madhvan Nair from Trivandrum, Sujatha Vaidyanathan from Chennai apart from three Chinese, one American and one Israeli graduate student and two PDFs one a British and the other a Japanese girl. It was a very cosmopolitan and informal get-together and Dr.and Mrs. Mitra were excellent hosts. The living room was very spacious, people were moving and constantly changing positions, they all knew each other well. Food and drinks were in plenty and everybody was enjoying the party. Nilanjana made acquaintances with all the Indian students and with Mrs. Suman Tripathi and Mrs. Deepa Majumdar and the party continued till well past midnight.

Nilanjana liked the social circle and both she and Sushovan enjoyed the evening. Sushovan had rented a two-roomed apartment near the institute. He had a Volkswagen 'Beetle' car from his Montreal days and Niranjana was experiencing her f rst winter and the snowfall in USA and was getting used to the way of life and cosmopolitan social grouping in America.

***

Manish had, by now, well settled into the groove of his working life. His brother-in-law had recently taken up a new job and the family had moved over to Phoenix in Arizona. Manish had started to go for morning walks regularly, heading for Central Park, the section which was less crowded and also had more forested hills than the part of it further south. He entered the Park through the pedestrian entrance bounded by walls of dark red stone block. Like most of the walkers and runners, he walked around the reservoir. There was a small playground on 100th Street (W) where mostly mothers and nannies with small children and infants in perambulators used to come in the evenings. He used to play basketball for a while after returning from the off ce in the evenings in the court on 86th street nearer his house. A tall muscular black American – Robert was the coach and he taught Manish the basics of the game. Robert was a health freak and used to regularly run in Central Park in the mornings. Gradually they became good friends and in fact, he induced Manish to regularly come for morning walks.

Robert was a few years older than him, was single, lived with his parents and a younger brother and worked with the Fire Services Deptt. Manish came to know the black American way of life mainly through him and found that they had much stronger family bonds than white Americans, which was much similar to the Indian families. After basketball in the evenings, they often used to come together as Robert used to live a few houses further away in House No 132. Manish often used to call him for a cup of tea together before Robert went to his house and their friendship f ourished. Within a few months, they became aware of each other's sexual preferences and they developed a liaison, Robert became his lover. However, both of them were very discreet about their special bonding, Manish because of his guilt complex of being in a sinful relationship and Robert because he had grown up in the locality and was now a respectable person.

***

Kamlesh went to the University in Syracuse. After getting the support from her parents, she was now quite determined. Bipasha's letter had shown her the direction. Yes! the f rst thing, she had to stand on her own feet. She loitered in the campus for a while, looking for some Indian faces from where to start the enquiry but could not f nd any. She saw the cafeteria, it was around lunchtime and she needed someplace to sit and rest. She went inside and as it was self-service, stood in the queue, picked up a coffee and a sandwich and looked around for a table to sit. At the far corner, she saw two girls looking like Indians, having their lunch. She went with her tray to the table and sat down beside them. After a while, the girl opposite her enquired" you seem to be a new face, are you a grad student here?

This provided the opening Kamlesh was looking for, she replied: "yes, I am new to this university but I am not yet a student". Then she introduced herself and said "I was sitting alone in my house downtown and felt like seeing the university. I am newly married and have come to USA only a few months back and my husband is on tour" she played safe.

The girls started talking, they both were graduate students, the one talking to her was Mrinalini Sharma from Allahabad and the other Sunita Reddy from Hyderabad. Sunita asked her "what does your husband do?"

"He is an engineer".

Sunita informed her that they were staying together in a rented house along with another girl and doing their light housekeeping. They wanted to sit for some more time but Mrinalini looked at her watch and said: "please excuse us, we have a class in ten minutes". Then they exchanged addresses and telephone numbers, the girls seemed to be quite social and easy going. Kamlesh invited them for lunch on the following Sunday at her house and they accepted. Sunita asked "if you don't mind, can we bring our friend Shabana also who stays with us?

Kamlesh agreed and they left for their classes.

On Saturday Kamlesh went to the bank and upon enquiry found that her father had sent $500 in her account which was more than suff cient to meet her expenses for more than a month provided she could get a cheaper accommodation. She made a mental note to enquire with the girls when they come to her house, withdrew some money, purchased grocery and went home in a happier frame of mind.

-28-

Arora sent Harish to his native village near Jalandhar and asked him to stay there till the case was settled. On the next date of hearing, his lawyer Negi took an adjournment, pleading that what had transpired was really an altercation between the two parties and soon it went out of control. It was a case of the sudden f ght and the intention was not to kill. Thus it should be registered, in fact as a case of culpable homicide not amounting to murder. The judge accepted his plea and the next date of hearing was f xed after two months. Arora was very happy as this in the eyes of law, was a lessor crime and its punishment also being lighter in comparison. Arora took Negi also this time to meet the night watchman's wife.

The wife was very happy to see Arora and complained that she had not yet received any compensation from the college as assured by him. Arora promised to look into the matter and enquired whether her two sons were back in the school to which she replied with folded hands "Saheb, because of your generosity not only my sons are going to school but the business in my shop has also considerably increased "and proudly showed her well-stuffed store. As a businessman, Arora knew well the value of money for the hard-pressed people and offered her another thousand rupees to meet her expenses until the compensation from the college was made available to her. She accepted the money with humility and thanked him, touching the money to her forehead. Arora asked her "what will you do with the money received from the college?"

She replied "This cottage needs major repairs urgently before the rainy season and also running water and electricity connection. I am very eagerly waiting for the money".

Arora then introduced Negi to her saying that he was the lawyer f ghting her case and Negi told her in the local dialect "he is the unfortunate father of the boy who had hit your husband out of fear of getting caught while returning from the night show and I am f ghting the case in the court of Shimla to see that proper justice is done to you".

The moment Negi uttered the sentence, she became very hostile and stood up to drive away Arora from her doorstep but Negi took her aside and in a low tone and said "see, you have two young sons to look after, the father is a good man as you must have already seen and he is very repentant for the misdeed of his son. Whatever has happened has happened, your husband is not coming back. Suppose I ask him to build a pucca two-roomed brick house for you and your sons, with toilet and kitchen along with tap water facility and electricity connection, will that satisfy you?"

The poor woman could not believe him as it was beyond her imagination, it was what they had dreamed since long but could not afford. She softened instantly and asked "Do you think he will agree to it? And looked at Arora.

Negi replied "let me try"

He took Arora side, talked to him in a low tone for about f ve minutes and then came back. Arora came forward to her with folded hands and said with all humility "I know what my son has done is unpardonable. He has already been rusticated from the college and his whole career has been ruined. But as a father I cannot abandon him, I will have to take care of him also. I will do what you are asking and what Vakil Saheb is instructing me to do but I have only one request to you and that is "you will kindly withdraw the case against my son from the police."

Negi took the woman aside and explained to her "you will not get a better deal. If his son goes to jail, it is not going to help you in any way. You also do not know how much compensation the college will give you and when. But if your pucca house is built with the generosity of this man, you can live happily for your whole life and use the compensation from the college for your future. I feel this is a very fair deal. What do you say?" he looked at her.

She kept thinking for some time and then asked: "When does he build the house?"

Negi talked to Arora and then came back "After he receives the letter from you. I stand guarantee for the house." He gave her his card, she had seen his new big house and this assured her. Negi told her "I will prepare the letter and will come back to you after f fteen days. You make up your mind by that time and if you agree, I promise that your house construction work will start within two weeks from the date of your signing the letter. The woman looked satisf ed and both Arora and Negi went away.

Arora asked Negi to prepare a cost estimate, with a break up of material cost as well as labour cost at the local rates plus the cost of extending the water pipeline and electricity line to his house and send it to him within a week. Negi agreed "I have built my new house only last year, I will ask my contractor to give a very reliable and reasonable rate" and they parted.

***

Nandini's recovery as it turned out was only temporary. Within a few months, the fever came back and the voice also became hoarse. During check-up in AIIMS, the doctors feared that cancer had spread in the gastrointestinal tract and advised to admit her in the ward without any further loss of time. She was admitted the next day. Doctors found that cancer had spread to the small intestine and she was operated upon next week to remove that portion of the intestine. The recovery took about two weeks but the fever did not subside Doctors diagnosed that the throat portion was aff icted, this time the tracheal portion. Radiation therapy continued for a month but not much improvement could be seen. The patient started losing weight rapidly and became very weak. Indrani and Sukriti came to see her and were shocked. She had become very weak and the lustre of life it seems had gone out from her face. Nandini could hardly talk and that also in a whispering tone. She could not take any solid food and be administered liquid food through a pipe inserted into her food pipe. The doctors felt that from here on the medicines and treatments were not to be of much help, it would only prolong the agony. Cancer had advanced to the terminal stage and the patient had a life expectancy of hardly two months. By now Nandini also had come to know that cancer had reached the terminal stage, she did not want to die in hospital and started asking her husband and others to take her home. Her pain was unbearable.

She used to moan constantly with tears rolling down her cheeks. She wanted to end her life soon to get rid of the misery. There was no point to prolong it any further, let her go with some dignity of life still left, she constantly prayed to God. One night during the doctor's round she had asked the doctor "why can't you terminate my life quickly, there is no point in my continuing this sort of life indef nitely."

The doctor had heard such dialogue many times from his terminally ill cancer patients. He knew the futility of the efforts to keep her alive but was bound by rules. He gave his standard reply" No, madam, euthanasia is still not legally permitted. As doctors, we are supposed to do our best to keep the patient alive and not kill him or her."

Nandini asked "but why? Even after knowing that it is a terminal case? Why should a body be subjected to such inhuman pain and suffering? Can I not be allowed some dignity while dying?

The Doctor was helpless and only said "the law does not permit it but on the optimistic side, some miracle might still happen and walked away.

Nandini insisted on her husband to take her home at the earliest. Agrawal discussed with doctors and they also felt that since medicines etc. had ceased to be of any help, there was no point in keeping the patient in the hospital, she could be taken home to fulf l her last wish. Agrawal arranged to engage a nurse - at home and brought her back to her home after more than two months in the hospital. By now, her two elder daughters who had come, in turns, to attend to her and had returned. Reema, her youngest daughter had come now and received her at home.

-29-

R obert was having his evening session in the house of Manish and they were talking. Robert was much more open about his sexual preference and told Manish 'believe me! I didn't choose to be gay. I was born with my feelings just like all other human beings."

This was in sharp contrast to the feelings of Manish who used to feel very guilty and sinful about the way he was. Whereas he took every care to keep his real sexuality under wraps, Robert it seemed, got a kick out of f aunting it and often used to say "look bro, this guilt feeling may perhaps be embedded in your cultural bringing up, but in this country, the gays are organizing to f ght out this discriminatory behaviour of the majority. We want to be treated like normal human beings and not as lepers or an outcast. We feel our sexuality should not make any difference in the matters of dealings of other people with us in day to day life."

Manish asked, "Do you think that even in this open country, one would face discrimination based on our sexuality?" Robert replied sarcastically "Don't fool yourself with the public face of this great US. of A. I am a law graduate but I could not continue in the law profession. The moment I revealed my sexual inclinations, I was made to clearly understand that I was unwanted in their respectful society. Likewise, teaching, banking, f nance etc - the so-called respectable jobs went out of bounds for me. This society will hound you out like lepers, the moment they know about it."

Manish argued, "if you already know that, it is simply much safer not to let people know about your sexual orientation."

Robert was introspective "may be what you say is more practical, I could probably have passed undetected, but that would be tantamount to be living my life as a lie and I do not like hypocrisy."

For the f rst time in life, Manish felt that he could discuss his abnormal state of sexuality and its problems with somebody. He asked, "Do your family members know about your sexual feelings?". "See, at f rst I didn't tell them rather I kept it hidden from them but three years back my mom started pestering me about marrying some girl she knew and felt would be a good match for me. She introduced the girl also to me with the hope that I would like her. It was at that point that I had to tell the truth to my dad and he understood. I told the truth to the girl as well, she was hurt initially but then she accepted it and since then we are good friends."

Manish said "similar thing had happened once to me also back home. She was a beautiful girl, had disrobed herself, I touched her breast and private parts also but believe me I had no reaction and felt so guilty and ashamed about the whole thing for months and kept thinking it was some kind of def ciency or plain impotence and since in our conservative society homosexuality is seen as an abominable crime, I could not discuss this with anybody." Robert commented "So! that proves my point that you don't choose your sexuality, rather are born with it just like other people around you, who don't choose their heterosexuality but are born with those feelings and I hope you understand what I mean" and Manish nodded.

Robert often used to take Manish to Brooklyn to meet other friends in a bar, frequented mostly by gays. They used to commute there by subway and Robert used to introduce Manish as his 'companion', as it was euphemistically called, the equivalent of 'girlfriend' so to say. Manish met in the bar many white and black people, all gays and for the f rst time in life, he felt as if he had entered in a world of like-minded people where he did not have to pretend his sexuality.

Manish received an urgent call from his sister Raashi that their father had a severe heart attack and he very much wanted to see Manish. So he f ew home by f rst available f ight and reached Delhi on the third day. Parashar was now past seventy and was also very much overweight. Since Anupam had been looking after the stores quite well, he had stopped going there and spent his whole time at home. He had a massive heart attack while climbing the stairs of his f at which was on the second f oor. Manish went to Batra hospital where his father was admitted and was taken to the I.C.U. Parashar recognized his son but since he was very weak, could not talk to him. Manish pressed his hands and got only a weak response.

Pasricha died on the f fth day in the hospital. Both the brothers performed the last rites and after all the rituals were over, her mother called both the sons. She asked Manish "Beta, you are now well past thirty, your father very much wanted to see you married so that we can think about the marriage of Anupam also."

Manish replied, "Ma, to tell you the truth, I want to settle down in USA and I don't have any plans to get married immediately so you can f x Anupam's marriage any time you want."

She was not ready for this "No, no! that doesn't look nice, people would ask why the elder brother does not want to get married."

Manish replied, "I will take some more time to settle down there and besides that since you are also getting old, you also need a helping hand to share the household work." He asked Anupam "if you have any preference, you tell mother and get married quickly. Your honeymoon trip would be fully sponsored by me, so tell me where do you want to go?"

Anupam promptly replied "Ooty." Manish said "done! get married quick, I will send you the tickets as well as hotel reservations. Do take care of the mother and the house." Manish f ew back to New York the next day.

***

On Sunday the girls came to Kamlesh. Mrinalini introduced the third girl as Shabana Warsi. She was born and brought up in USA as her parents were from Boston and were USA. Citizens who had emigrated from Bihar in the 1960s. Shabana had almost completed her Ph.D. in Economics and was waiting for her thesis to be submitted, she was in Syracuse for the last four years. Mrinalini and Sunita were in their second year of graduate studies. Kamlesh had already prepared the lunch and all of them ate with great relish. After lunch, while they were having ice cream, the girls were going through the photo album while

Kamlesh was preparing coffee in the kitchen and was contemplating as to how to broach the subject. When she came out of the kitchen she found the girls whispering something among themselves. On seeing her Shabana asked, showing her marriage photograph, the name of her husband and she told. Shabana seemed shocked and exclaimed, "how this is possible?".

Kamlesh asked "what?"

Shabana was not like any other Indian girl, she was born and brought up in USA. She decided to be blunt and direct "this fellow is already married. I have seen him along with his wife and kid in Mr. Bhangu's house, both are colleagues in the same off ce" and looked at Kamlesh.

The curtain was down for Kamlesh. In a way it was good, she did not have to f nd a way to tell it. For a long time she remained silent and then faced the" I knew this only after coming to USA" and she, with tears rolling down her eyes and sobbing, then told them the whole story. The lightheartedness of the atmosphere changed abruptly and all the girls, who were more or less of the same age became very pensive. Shabana asked. "What have you decided to do now?". "My parents are asking me to come back to India but I want to stand on my own feet here, continue my studies and become a graduate student like you ultimately."

Sunita said, "but for that, you have to pass the required qualifying exams and it will take some time." Kamlesh said, "but the most immediate problem is that I will have to leave this f at by the month-end and I would need your help in f nding cheaper accommodation." She looked at them.

They looked at each other and then Shabana said 'you can move to our place and stay in my room. I should be able to submit my thesis within a month or month and a half at most after that I would leave for Boston and then you can stay on there" she looked at the other two girls for approval. They immediately gave their consent and Mrinalini said:" In that case, you can move in with us on the coming weekend."

Kamlesh was very grateful for this generous offer from them but Shabana said: " as fellow human beings that is the least we could do but let me tell you the goal you are choosing is not easy and there will be a long struggle ahead."

Kamlesh only said, "my circumstances have brought me here and to regain my self-respect, I guess I have no other choice and so I want to give it a try."

All the three girls in unison said "and count us in also in your efforts. We will be with you in getting you out of this situation. Just feel free to move in with us."

This was a great first step that Kamlesh desperately needed to come out of not only her loneliness but from all past associations of her life with Prem. She decided to vacate the apartment and informed her landlady accordingly. Suddenly her zest for a living started coming back and she started dreaming of a better future. With all her heart she wanted to make a fresh start in life, moved in with other girls on the next weekend and informed her parents accordingly. Her father wanted her to file a case for divorce in the local court and agreed to fully finance her to fight it. He wanted her to find a good lawyer and also to find Prem's address in New York and other details about him, if possible as those would be needed during the case. However, thinking that she already had enough troubles of her own they did not tell her about the problems of Harish.

Kamlesh discussed filing a divorce case with her friends. Shabana volunteered to find out the details about Prem from Mr. Bhangu and also offered to find out the names of few lawyers who could·help her in fighting the case.

-30-

Negi telephoned Arora that the watchman's wife had signed the documents in exchange for the house as promised and that had paved the way for an out of the court settlement which he felt, should be acceptable to the court. He also sent the cost estimate for the construction of the house with a front Verandah, one room, kitchen, toilet on the ground f oor and one room Verandah, some roof space on the f rst f oor and a staircase going down. He also gave a time frame along with the cost of water and electricity connection. Arora made some small addition to it by converting the front Verandah into a provision stores with wooden racks on around two sides to keep the provisions, a counter and wooden planks to lock the stores from inside along with entrance to house from the other side of the verandah, complete with boundary fencing with barbed wire and a front gate for entrance to the compound.

On the next date of hearing the government advocate pleaded his arguments for awarding maximum punishment to the accused. Negi in his turn submitted his documents for an out of court settlement. The judge summoned the wife of the deceased watchman to know whether she agreed to whatever was written in the document and had been signed by her and on getting her consent after explaining what was written in it, gave a new date for the next hearing. Arora requested the watchman's family to shift to some adjacent place so that the construction activity could be started.

The whole family seemed very excited and shifted to the makeshift shanty made by the contractor in a few days. Arora himself was a building contractor, gave the necessary instructions to the local contractor along with initial advance payment, paid the family another f ve hundred rupees to meet their day to day expenditure, requested the college authorities to release her compensation and asked Negi to look after the other details of the case before returning back to Delhi.

Partho completed his B.Tech from I.I.T. Roorkee and got campus appointment from Wipro, Bangalore and joined there. Santanu retired from service from EIL and joined a consultancy f rm in the private sector in Nehru Place. Bipasha was by now in the second year of her Ph.D studies. Her research guide Prof. Thukral was a very busy person and had therefore assigned the job of the day to day supervision of her research work to his post-doctoral student Dr. Anshrman Bist who had done his Ph.D. two year back with Prof. Thukral. Dr. Bist was a very amiable person, was a Garhwali from Chamba and had been a brilliant student. For her day to day work, Bipasha had been taking all instructions from Dr. Bist and through a close professional association, they started coming nearer, which slowly got converted into mutual attraction. They often used to go to the departmental canteen for tea, he helped her in preparing the material for the departmental seminar apart from overseeing her day to day progress and they were also often seen together in the library.

Nandini's condition was now deteriorating very fast. She had become very weak and completely bedridden. A nurse used to take her care from 8 am to 8 pm and during the night Reema used to sit by her bedside up to midnight and thereafter Agrawal used to sit till the nurse came. By now Nandini's voice had also gone and she could make only some guttural sound, mostly talking only in sign language. It very much pained Agrawal to see his wife lying in such helpless condition and inching slowly to death and yet he could not do anything to mitigate her pain. Doctors had said she had a life span of four or f ve more weeks. She was being fed through a tube, was having a constant fever, was given medicines regularly but without any discernible effect. She was having constant pain which used to become unbearable at times when she used to writhe with pain and tears would f ow from her eyes.

By the end of two weeks, she had lost more than half her weight and became light as a child. By the third week, her body started to rot starting from the throat and a stench of rotten f esh f lled up the room, so much so that the nurse refused to sit in her room except for administering her medicines, giving her food or changing her catheter or for cleaning her. Nandini had almost lost all her consciousness by now.

Agrawal was sitting by her side at dead of the night and could hardly look at her. With open eyes, she was looking at him as if pleading to free her from the misery of leading such an undignif ed life. He prayed to God for an early end of her life and did not know when he had fallen asleep on his chair's handle. He dreamt that he and Nandini had gone to some hill station but Nandini had become a small child. They were walking through a wood with large Pine trees when suddenly a Python coming from somewhere caught hold of her feet and started to swallow her. She started shrieking, writhing with pain and was being swallowed slowly and up to her belly while Agrawal was watching helplessly around. Suddenly a voice from heaven commanded, "the only way to free her from the clutches of the Python is to shoot her and do it right away." He shot her in the head obeying the command and behold! She immediately was transformed into a bird, freed herself, f ew away into the sky and he kept watching her till she disappeared in the distant horizon. Looking down he was astonished to see that the snake was burning with a sooty f ame and was soon reduced into a pile of ashes. Agrawal woke up suddenly, looked around and saw that Nandini was looking approvingly at him as if she had witnessed the scene and was smiling. He got up with a determination, took the towel kept on top of the bed, put it on her nose and smothered her lightly. After a few moments there was a slight movement of her head, then feet and then she became still. He lifted the towel kept it back on top of the bed and in a low tone said, "Goodbye, my dear wife for the last 45 years, I could not bear your pain any more! God please forgive me or give me any punishment you want and tears rolled down his eyes. He went back to his chair, fell asleep into a deep slumber till he was woken up by his daughter Reema in the morning. She was crying and informed him "mother has died during the night." In a while, the nurse also came and conf rmed the death. It was a great relief for all of them as the patient's suffering was unbearable, only death could bring her the deliverance from pain!

-31-

Manish and Robert often went together to the Brooklyn Bar where they used to meet other gay people. It was a new experience for Manish to see so many other people like him and his sense of guilt about his abnormal sexuality began to recede. Robert or Bobby as he was called by his friends, seemed to be quite familiar with most of them and introduced Manish to his other friends, both black and white. One of them was Simon, of Dutch parentage but born and brought up in New York, whose father had landed in New York about forty-f ve years back as an immigrant and was now running a restaurant in Brooklyn. Simon had done his masters from Columbia University, had been a teacher for the f rst few years but later found that due to his gay orientation, he was not acceptable to the society and was forced to leave the job because the principal feared he would be a bad inf uence on the students. Manish asked "what did you do then?"

"So I started assisting my dad in running the restaurant. After the death of my father three years back, now I am running it, assisted by my younger brother."

Simon was a travel addict. He had hitchhiked across the US and Canada and took a month or two off every year to travel around the world. He told Manish the good points about travelling very cheap so that it could be stretched to a much larger limit in travelling around the world. He was also a health freak and did not smoke nor drink. His companion was another white guy Philips by name but they were not steady and went out with others also. Simon invited Manish to join during his next travel trip to the Arab Countries in Africa during the Christmas holidays. All four were drinking beer together in the bar and the talk drifted to their sexuality. Manish asked "why did God create us gay. It is against nature. The whole creation is based on male-female union for the propagation of species, then why we have been deprived of our normal sexuality?"

Simon shrugged "we do not know, may be it is an aberration. Anyway, all the rules have exceptions and so may be our sexuality also".

Robert agreed "what you say may be true also. My one vet friend tells me that in the animal husbandry section of their dairy where the breeding is done, they have observed that may be about one per cent or so of the bulls, though they look very healthy, are simply not interested in the cows. So any attempts to induce them to mount the cows remain unsuccessful."

Philips enquired "so what happens to them?"

"They are replaced with other bulls who are willing." Simon commented, "may be they pair with other bulls?"

Robert Shrugged "may be, but I will ask my vet friend about this angle".

Manish said, "but the implication of this different sexual orientation means thereby that marriage, family, wife, children and things like that have got no meaning for us".

From there the discussions drifted to a more immediate topic. Simon in a low tone confessed" you see I have a lot of black friends and I am also quite open about my sexuality. May be due to these odd combinations, I see that police suspects me as a shady character."

Manish asked, "why do you think so?"

"You see, police keeps a watch on my activities, many a time they have stopped my car, have searched both me and the car, have followed me and my black friends and even searched my apartment during my absence".

Robert asked, "your parents must have objected?"

Simon clarif ed "No, I live alone in a rented apartment building f at, mostly populated by blacks and police many times do surprise checks during odd hours and twice have searched the house thoroughly even during my presence. They perhaps suspect that I am a drug peddlcr whereas I have never taken any drug. I am fed up with this attitude of NYPD (New York police Deptt.) Robert was infuriated "that is all the more reason why gay people have to collectively f ght against the unjust attitude of the society toward us. You see, next week there is going to be held a big rally organized by the "Gay Liberation Front" in the Times Square, you tell all your friends to be present there in big numbers and make our presence felt. Time has come when we have to come out in the open instead of hiding and f ght for our rights. We also have equal rights to live freely in this heterosexuality dominated society."

The rally next week turned out to be a grand success with more than f ve hundred participants, both black and white, shouting slogans with placards displaying "we are gay, God made us so," "we also have rights to live in this society as per our free choice." "Stop police harassment against us" etc. People spoke animatedly against gay discrimination and that it was not a crime to be gay. Simon spoke about the police harassment while Robert highlighted the fact that great many of the so-called respectable professions treat them as a pariah because of the prejudice of the society against the gay, as a result, those professions have closed their doors to gays even though they have the qualif cations etc. The rally was well covered by media got good coverage in evening T.V. news, the printed media also gave it space. The rally of the gay people made an impact on the society, it seemed, at least people started accepting the existence of gay people in the society, as a result, they gained some visibility.

***

Kamlesh had now been living with the girls of her age group who were shaping their futures and this gave her conf dence to face her misfortune. In the company of the girls, she had a temporary sense of security but these girls were busy with their academic pursuits and she was feeling a void in her life. Her father had insisted that she should share the expenditure incurred with the girls for the housekeeping and that she did, but her own life seemed to be devoid of any meaning. For the f rst few months, the injustice done to her to ruin her life remained uppermost in her mind to make her very emotionally disturbed. Shabana found out the details about Prem from Mr. Bhangu, who clarif ed that Prem was not his colleague but a junior subordinate in an associate company, which lent their workers during winter months temporarily to the main company and gave Kamlesh the name of his off ce in Syracuse, his off ce address in New York and its telephone numbers, his residence telephone number in New York and address and also the fact that initially though he had joined the master's Programme in Syracuse university but since he could not make the grade in the exams so had to leave after a year. He had to take up some construction job of a lower rung because he did not have a degree from USA, in the diff cult territories of Alaska near Fairbanks where people were not prepared to go. During the harsh winter in Alaska, the company moved most of its construction f eld staff to New York and called them back at the start of summer. While in Alaska he had married some waitress working in a bar and that had helped him in getting the US Citizenship quickly.

With the help of the lawyer arranged by Shabana, she had f led a case of bigamy against Prem in the Syracuse court, which issued him a summon. Prem appeared in the court and submitted an aff davit through his lawyer thus: "I had given temporary shelter to this hapless woman out of pity because she claimed that she had freshly arrived from India and knew nobody in Syracuse. She is not my wife, I am already married to an American woman. This woman is trying to trap me, is loose and with the consent of my wife, we have decided to sever any further relationship with this woman." That was Prem's f rst and last appearance in court and after that, he did not come at all. the next Summon sent by the Court for his appearance was returned from the address as not traceable. Shabana found out from Mr. Bhangu that Prem had gone back to Alaska along with other f eld staff with the advent of summer. Her lawyer advised Kamlesh to retain a copy of the aff davit, duly attested by the court, as a legal proof that Prem had refused to accept her Hindu marriage to him so that he could never blackmail her.

However her lawyer could not nail Prem as he was a US citizen and the so-called marriage with Kamlesh had not been performed on US soil, neither had it been registered (as most of the Hindu marriages in India are not registered in court anyway). Living with another woman for a while with her consent was not considered against law, thus as per the US laws prevalent in the land, there was no legal basis to proceed against the accused. Prem escaped the hands of the law in spite of the best efforts of Aroras and this added to the frustration and a sense of defeat of Kamlesh. Whatever the outcome, the legal proceedings in

US turned out to be very expensive and to meet the legal expenses at the US end, Poonam had to sell her beauty Parlour at Alkapuri market though she did not tell it to her daughter.

Shabana in the meantime submitted her thesis and moved back to Boston to her parents. The girls were very sympathetic to her but in retrospect Kamlesh felt that if her case was so weak, she should not have gone to the court in the f rst place, the collateral damage being that the court case had generated a lot of unwanted publicity to her misfortune and she shunned any contacts with the Indian community.

Time, however, is a great healer. Kamlesh was forced now to look forward only, her past being a nightmare which she wanted to forget. Both Sunita and Mrinalini advised her to be f nancially independent as a f rst step if she wanted to live in this country. But Sunita said, "She can not get any job here because of her visa status."

Mrinalini agreed but was still optimistic "but various agencies need some temporary helping hands from time to time for doing many kinds of odd jobs" and looked at Kamlesh "are you agreeable to do the menial jobs also?"

Kamlesh replied, "Do I have any choice?" Mrinalini said "Not much. I guess you have no job experience also, so you have to start from somewhere and that also from nearer to the bottom of the ladder." Kamlesh gave her consent. "I am ready" and that settled the matter.

In their block, there was a job available for a baby sitter. She went there and found that the employer was a single parent a divorced mother who worked in an off ce and had a f ve-year-old school-going daughter, who came back from the school at three in the afternoon whereas the mother returned at six in the evening. Kamlesh had to be present in the house in this time gap, feed the child and take care of her till she returned. This was a three hour per day job, f ve days a week and she was to be paid every week as per the prevailing rates. Kamlesh accepted the job. The earning was enough to meet her share of housekeeping and it also kept her busy. At the end of the month, she asked her father to stop sending money to her as she had got a job.

After about two months Sunita informed that there was an immediate vacancy for a dishwasher in the university cafeteria and asked Kamlesh to meet the Cafetaria manager the very next day. She went there and found that the job was for three hours per day from eleven to two O'clock f ve days a week including free lunch. Kamlesh got the job and wanted to leave the babysitting job but the mother requested her to continue for some more time as her daughter seemed to like her and so Kamlesh retained both the jobs. The dishwashing job was a hard one, a large member of dishes had to be cleaned, washed, dried and stacked. After f nishing her work and lunch, Kamlesh had to straightaway go for the babysitting job which was however not very taxing as by now she had developed a friendly relationship with the kid.

Kamlesh liked the job in the university, it was a hard job but it allowed her to come back to a familiar environment of students. She was happy for the f rst time after coming to the USA and checked the procedure to get into graduate school. Sunita informed "you have to pass GRE (Graduate Record Examination) and TOEFL (an English prof ciency test), as English is not your mother tongue. We have got admission here after clearing both from India."

Kamlesh started preparing for the GRE and TOEFL in her spare time in morning and evenings and thus became very busy for the f rst time after coming to USA.

<h1 style="text-align:center">-32-</h1>

On his next visit to Solan, Arora found that the construction of the house was going on well and the watchman's family was quite happy to see the progress. On seeing him the wife informed "I have received the compensation from the college through it is less than what I had expected "Arora consoled her "anyway, it is good that you have ultimately got it" and then enquired "how are your sons doing in the school?"

At this, the elder son came forward and told "I have passed in all the subjects in the half-yearly exams and so has my younger brother" and presented his younger brother to the fore. Arora touched their heads in a gesture of blessing and told the elder son "you have to look after your mother and the family, so pay your full attention to the studies."

Negi told him that the judge had accepted his plea for an out of the court settlement and only the police had to be persuaded to withdraw the FIR and Arora agreed to give them suff cient inducement for doing so. The case was fully settled after one more of his visits to Solan and Harish was exonerated. The house was also ready in the meantime and the watchman's family shifted to their new double-storeyed house complete with kitchen, running water, electricity and toilet facilities. The front verandah, with due modif cations, was converted into a provision store with shelves, counter and arrangements to close and lock the front portion with collapsible grill and wooden planks. Arora gave the wife another one thousand rupees to stuff the store with provisions and returned to Delhi fully satisf ed. He called Harish back from and asked him to help him in running the business.

***

Kamlesh was continuing with her babysitting job and had developed good rapport not only with the daughter Pamela but also with her mother Amanda, who was in her early thirties. Often Kamlesh will prepare tea for her after she came back from off ce and have tea and snacks together as well as chit chat for a while. Amanda was a Chartered accountant and told her that she was married to a lawyer but later he turned into an alcoholic, was thrown out of the job and started cheating on her and so she divorced him. It was better, she felt, to remain single rather than having a rogue husband. Gradually Kamlesh also opened her heart to Amanda and they became friends. In next six months or so Kamlesh cleared the TOEFL and GRE and was admitted as a graduate student in the university w.e.f. the next fall i.e. September session, along with a scholarship. This was dream come true for her, Mrinalini and Sunita threw a party to celebrate the occasion and Kamlesh invited Amanda and Pamela also to it to share her joy as she was going to start a new life within a few months. Amanda congratulated Kamlesh though she was sorry that in a few months she had to lookout for a new baby sitter. Kamlesh wrote a long letter to Bipasha and thanked her profusely for advising her to stay on and resume her studies.

Sushovan had phoned Indrani earlier and had told about his plan to go to Montreal in April with Nilanjana for his convocation and Bipasha was very keen to talk to her mama (mother's brother), so Indrani handed over the receiver to her daughter. After the preliminary pleasantries, Bipasha asked about his tour details and Sushovan informed "Montreal is about four hundred miles away and we have decided to go by our car. I have also booked a room in Y.M.C.A. there for three days and Nilanjana is quite excited about the trip as this would be our f rst long drive in USA."

Bipasha enquired "Mama, my closest friend Kamlesh lives in Syracuse, does that place come on the way?"

"Well! not exactly, the normal route is via Albany, but there is also a longer route via Syracuse. Why? Any special message?"

She said, "you have guessed it right, the message is indeed there but you have to promise that you will meet her."

Sushovan agreed "well if you are so keen ..." Bipasha interrupted "yes, I am very keen". "In that case, I will have to change my travel plan a bit. While going I will drive straight to Montreal but while coming back, we will make a stopover at Syracuse and meet your friend. O.K! now what is the message?" asked Sushovan.

"I will not tell you. You please f nish your talk with ma and then handover the phone to Niludi er........Nilu Mamima" and handed over the phone to her mother. In a while, Indrani went away and handed over the receiver to her. Nilanjana was on the line at the other end" so, what is the secret message I have to pass on to your friend. Your mama is not in the room and you may talk freely." "The message is that you will bring her with you to spend a few days in New Jersey. She deserves some break from her routine life and you will give her the break."

She then told her the story of Kamlesh and how she was struggling to come up in life and make a separate identity for herself but cautioned. "Do not try to show any pity on her for her misfortune, it may alienate her. Be quite normal to her."

Nilanjana replied, "I promise!"

Bipasha then gave her the telephone number of Kamlesh and asked "please f rm up the dates and other details with her and let me know when you call us next time. I have already told her about you two."

Accordingly, Nilanjana telephoned Kamlesh, introduced herself and f rmed up the dates etc. and Kamlesh was happy with the proposal. Nilanjana informed Bipasha accordingly.

Lopamudra was due to retire from the Rajagiri School soon, after more than twenty years of service. Nilanjana was quite happy in US now and Indraneel had just cleared his chartered accountancy and so her liabilities were f nally over. She was given a very emotional farewell by her colleagues in School and her close friends gave her a farewell dinner in the Chopstick restaurant in the Asiad village. After retirement she suddenly had a great feeling of loneliness in life, Indranil was away from the house most of the time because of his new job. To keep herself busy, she started to take some tuition at home and also started giving her voluntary services in Chittaranjan Memorial library, of which she was a very old member, for two hours daily in the evening.

-33-

A major tragedy struck Robert suddenly. In a practice game, another player collided with him and he fell with a heavy thud, two other players falling over him and he bruised himself badly over two-three places, one on his knees with a deep cut. For the f rst few days, he did not pay much attention after cleaning the bruises with anti-septic and applying the medicine from the First Aid Kit. In a week, the bruises got infected, f lled with pus and swelling all around, accompanied by fever. He consulted a doctor who cleaned the wounds, gave antibiotic tablets and asked him to come after f ve days. But the antibiotics had no effect and the infection not only continued but increased along with the fever. He had to take leave from his off ce. The doctor was puzzled, asked him to get his blood tested and referred him to a specialist in Jewish General Hospital.

In the hospital thorough pathological tests were done, Robert was diagnosed to have the dreaded AIDS, was admitted in the isolated ward where his condition went from bad to worse and he died after three weeks. Manish and Simon used to go to see him and the doctors after knowing their case histories advised them to get their blood tested and both of them tested HIV positive. Manish became very scared but the doctor said "If you keep taking the medicines regularly and lead an active and regular life, there is no reason that you will not have the normal life span. However, you have to be very careful to avoid sex with a normal person or mouth to mouth contact or mixing of blood with other people because you must remember all the time that you are the carriers of AIDS and have the full potentials to infect others." He gave them a plastic card, duly f lled up, and insisted them to show the card to the Pharmacist whenever they went for any medicine, check-ups or treatment.

The news of his vulnerability and the loss of Robert not only shattered Manish but restricted his life very much to avoid intimate contact with normal persons. There was a great stigma attached to HIV and AIDS in the society everywhere since AIDS was f rst reported in 1981 and the situation was still scary in the late 1990s. Earvin 'Magic' Johnson, the thirty-two-year-old basketball legend in the peak of his career had informed the world of his HIV infection in 1991.

The misconceptions about the disease that it was restricted to the gays, drug users and sex workers were still prevalent. Thus being infected with HIV was considered equivalent to being awarded the death sentence, as a progression from HIV to full-blown AIDS was only considered a matter of time. The doctors could not predict any time frame but could only say that the progression to AIDS could be delayed with the help of proper (and quite expensive) medicines, a nutritious diet and regular exercise.

The long list of medicines which his doctor had prescribed and which he had to keep taking life long, were to remain very expensive and he had to have suff cient income to meet his medical expenses. This coupled with the other requirements meant that he had to have a level of income which would not be possible in India and this precluded any possibility of his return ever to India. He had no choice but to settle down in USA permanently. Externally there would be no visible change but the new realization meant that he could not any more be casual or callous about his way of life. The doors to marriage, kids, the family had already been closed to him and now all normal social interactions also were to be restricted and life was mostly to remain conf ned to the gay circle. He kept going to the Brooklyn Bar and continued his associations with friends.

Simon was going on his annual vacations to the Arab countries during Christmas and he invited Manish to join him. Manish was already feeling very depressed and also wanted to see the world and so gave his consent. Simon told him not to be unduly worried about his HIV positive status as he was HIV positive for the last f ve years and was still hale and hearty. The only change he had made was that he had started living separately from his family. Simon told him that as they were now going to Africa, they had to take vaccinations for yellow fever and cholera. Apart from that tourist visa formality for different countries had to be completed, American express Traveller's Cheques had to be got made and also a rucksack and also a sleeping bag had to be purchased for travelling light and for not looking very distinguished. Manish asked, "what is this problem of not looking very distinguished?" Simon explained "See, we are going to Africa i.e. the third world. Americans are known the world over as stinking rich fellows, so you stand a good chance of being robbed at remote places."

Manish nodded "I get you"

He continued "More important thing is that these countries are mostly French-speaking, so I have already joined a French class and I will advise that you also join it soon" and Manish agreed. Within a week Manish found a centre giving French lessons near his off ce and joined the classes for two hours in the evening f ve days a week. Simon also arranged to get made two International student cards on the strength of being students in the French class.

Manish asked, "why student's card?"

"This will entitle us to avail student concession wherever possible and keep our travel cheap." With the help of the International student card, he made reservations in the YMCA Youth hostels, wherever they were available, as per his itinerary. Manish could see that Simon had made all preparations as an experienced traveller.

At the start of Christmas vacations, they started their voyage by a cargo ship with limited passenger accommodations economy class, from New York harbour. The ship was sailing to Cape Town, South Africa via the west coast of Africa, Casablanca being its f rst stop. They got down at Casablanca in Morocco and were now in Arab Africa, predominantly Muslim in culture. Simon had already made a reservation in the YMCA Youth hostel, which was located in the old part of the city. The youth hostel crowd mostly comprised young people just out of their teens, both boys and girls from West European countries, US and Canada. Some were f nishing their trip of Africa and going back to Europe or were coming from Europe and starting their trip to Africa after crossing the narrow Gibraltor Channel from Algeciras Spain by boat and landing in Africa at Ceuta in Morocco within an hour.

After the cold of New York, the winter seemed very mild in Africa. For Manish the food habits, the inhabitants, the dress of common people, burqua clad women, bazaars, haggling and bargaining etc. all reminded him of India and he could decidedly see that he had entered the third world as well as feel the difference in the culture. They stayed in the youth hostel for three days. Casablanca was the biggest city of Morocco on the Atlantic side of the sea and a big port. His knowledge of French was of much value here as people did not understand English. Morocco had been a French colony earlier. They started for the capital city of Rabat the next morning, got their visa for Algeria and Tunisia made, stayed in a hotel for the night and then proceeded to the old city of Fez where they had reservations in the youth hostel.

Many people from the crowd of a youth hostel in Casablanca were already there and they stayed in Fez, an old educational centre, for two days, went in a group to see the older part of the city called Medina built of mud walls and narrow lanes where the radios were blaring Hindi f lm songs. It seemed Hindi cinema was very popular in Morocco. The hitchhikers coming from the Algerian side told that vehicular traff c between the two countries was minimal as a result they faced great diff culty hitchhiking and it took a lot of time. To save time Simon and Manish took the aerial route to Algiers.

Algiers was the capital city of Algeria and was a beautiful port city, Algeria being the best colony of France. They stayed in a hotel for three days in Algeria. Simon wanted to see the famous Sahara desert and so was gathering information from two other boarders staying in the hotel with whom he had made acquaintance. Fortunately for him, they were going to Setif by car the next day and invited Simon also to come along with them up to Setif which was more than six hundred kilometres by road. On the last night during their stay in Algiers, Simon became the lover of Manish and from there on Manish became his companion. They travelled together up to Cairo for almost a month. This travel also developed a strong bond of friendship between both of them which was to last for their lifetime. They returned to New York from Cairo.

-34-

Sushovan and Nilanjana started for Montreal on a f ne Saturday morning in March. It was a bright sunny day, quite cold but enjoyable. They reached Albany before midday, had an early lunch, started onwards, had evening tea at Champlain, crossed the US border, reached Montreal by seven P.M. or so and checked into YMCA hotel. Next day was Sunday. Sushovan telephoned his research guide Prof. Gilman who invited them for dinner in his place in the evening. Sushovan told his wife that Canadians have their dinner by six in the evening and so they have to reach there early. They went out for sightseeing. He showed her the McGill University, the McIntyre building where he used to work, the three-storeyed brownstone house on the Bluerry street where he used to live. They were now on Sherbrooke (W) Boulevard and went to Plas Ville' Marie, the famous plaza of the town and sat in the bright sunshine under sun on the benches in the huge square, had lunch in the underground market of the plaza, came out on the St. Catharine boulevard parallel to Sherbrooke. They then leisurely walked east on St. Catherine and reached Place des Arts which had a huge auditorium for concerts, musical evenings or theatre etc. Below the auditorium was the underground Metro Station, in two levels, for east-west as well as North-South directions commuting. St. Catharine Boulevard was the shopping district having huge stores and shops on both sides of the road. Thereafter they returned to YMCA and after some rest went to Prof. Gilman's house.

Two of Sushovan's old colleagues were also invited for the dinner. Dr.Annie Weissmann was working as P.D.F. with the professor whereas Dr.Chandler was working in a pharmaceutical company. Sushovan introduced his wife with all of them and then they sat down for their social round of drinks. Annie was curious and asked "Suvan, (abbreviated form of Sushovan), you had said that you were going to Calcutta for marriage and were to join Allembic after your return, but seems you changed your plans midway, married a Delhi girl and joined as PDF in New Jersey, what happened?"

He pointed the f nger to his wife "All due to this girl I met in Delhi, she hijacked my plans "and looked at her. All eyes now turned to Nilanjana. Mrs. Gilman appreciatively looked at her "we all can see why you were hijacked but it does not explain why you rejected the offer from Alembic?"

Sushovan replied "that came as package deal"

Annie asked, "you mean she arranged the job for you?"

Sushovan clarif ed "No, no, not that. You see, she made it quite clear at the beginning itself that she did not want to settle down in Canada so either I had to return to India soon or I had to marry somebody else and I had to agree to her terms."

Dr. Gilman was curious and looked at Nilanjana "why? is Canada too cold or not good enough?"

Nilanjana shyly replied "my father died when I was very young and mother, as a single parent reared me up and my brother. I want to be near her when she becomes old and do my bit, if and when she needed some help". Both Dr. and Mrs. Gilman were very much moved and Mrs. Gilman asked "Are the children in India so much concerned about their old parents? How I wish our western society also retained these old world values!" Sushovan said "The modern generation back home also does not much care about these values any more but I was, anyway, f oored by her sentiments and instantly decided to come back soon and to be able to do that decided to do a stint of P.D.F. in the continent in order to join the academic profession there after a few years."

Dr. Chandler asked, "I don't get it, you mean the R&D set up in a pharmaceutical company is not considered good enough to get a job in India?" Sushovan immediately corrected him "No, no, the salary levels here are so high that it prevents you from going back and I look forward to a university teaching job in the long run."

Dr. Gilman agreed "you have made the right decision I feel. Here also the salary levels are higher in non-academic careers. It looks like she helped you in setting up your goals in life."

Mrs. Gilman opined "She has in her a good wife material" she stood up and asked Nilanjana and Annie to help her in setting up the dinner table.

The convocation ceremony was held the next day where Sushovan met his other old friends also. On the occasion, the old Alumni Association held a dinner followed by a cultural programme in the university auditorium. It was a busy day and Sushovan bade goodbyes to his old friends and returned to YMCA. Next morning, they started early for their return journey after breakfast, took the highway 401 far Ontario and continued upstream of St. Lawrence River. In two hours they crossed over to Ontario province, the scenic beauty was increasing as they were going east. Sushovan was explaining "St. Lawrence river originates from lake Ontario and as you may be knowing that lake Ontario, in turn, is connected to the other four great lakes of the American continent which in turn is connected to the Atlantic ocean. These lakes extend up to Winnipeg in Manitoba province. Thus the big ships from Atlantic ocean in the east coast enter into the continent through the St. Lawrence River. Montreal is a big port on the river, the ships continue to go all the way to up to Winnipeg, thus reaching the heartlands of the continent. Do you understand the signif cance of this?" he asked.

Nilanjana replied "must be very good for business purposes, I presume".

He nodded "that's right. St. Lawrence route system opens the heart of North America to ocean shipping during summer months, linking the oceans of the world with the great lakes of the American continent, thus benef tting both Canada as well as US"

They were now entering the Thousand Island area, straddled with a chain of big and small islands, stretching to about eighty km further upstream up to almost Kingston in Ontario. She was looking at the numerous islands on the river. He explained "Due to a large number of islands, this area of the river is known as Thousand Islands. One of the smallest islands is called 'Just Room Enough' consisting of a single house only and there is another island named Deer Island, owned by a secret society of Skull and Bones."

They had now left the Highway 401 and had taken Highway 137, heading for the thousand island bridge connecting Ontario in Canada to the New York State in US Wellesley island. They soon reached the Canadian border, crossed over to the US side and came over the bridge. The scenery was breathtaking, big, medium and small islands spread all around the wide river, made it very eye-catching. Due to the winter, everything was covered with snow, the river frozen, the sunshine falling over the surface making it look very bright. Nilanjana asked him to stop for a while and they enjoyed the scenic beauty from the bridge. On crossing the bridge they entered the Jefferson county and were now on Interstate 81 in the US They stopped for lunch in Watertown, then headed for Syracuse and reached at the address of Kamlesh by evening. She was waiting for them, had already taken leave from the employers, her friends had not yet come back from the university. After tea at her place, they started and reached New Jersey by eight or so.

Kamlesh was only a few years younger to Nilanjana and was meeting someone from her hometown for the f rst time during her stay in US She liked the couple and was touched by their warmth. At night Nilanjana telephoned Bipasha and surprised her by handing over the receiver to Kamlesh. Both were very happy to recognize each other's voice and were initially choked by emotion but soon overcame it, started talking and updated each other about the developments. Then Kamlesh handed over the Phone to Nilanjana who updated Bipasha about the Montreal trip. Bipasha asked her to let Kamlesh speak again to her next day a a lot of catching up was still to be done.

Next day Bipasha told Kamlesh about her great secret "looks like, I have fallen in love with a senior researcher in my deptt."

Kamlesh was immediately curious "tell me in detail", Bipasha told about Dr. Anshuman Bist and the romance going on between them concluding with "it, is still at the platonic plain only."

Kamlesh cautioned "Don't commit about your future unless you learn the details about his family and back history. From my experience, I can only say that I don't trust any man now."

Bipasha was in a confused state of mind and asked her opinion "See, our backgrounds are very different—I am Bengali and he is a Pahari chap, I am nonvegetarian and he is vegetarian, we come from different linguistic and cultural background also, do you think there can be a common future?"

Kamlesh said "my parents had arranged the marriage within our caste language and cultural background and you know what happened. I am not very sure about those factors any more. What primarily matters is how is the boy."

Bipasha asked, "so what do you advise me now?"

"If you feel that you both are getting serious, tell about your relationship to your parents, take him to them and ask uncle to independently f nd out about his past including his family."

Bipasha exclaimed, "how I wish that you would be here, you would have been the f rst person to whom I would introduce him."

Kamlesh heaved a sigh "Don't know when that would be possible, but count me in whatever way you decide".

Bipasha then updated her about Aroras and also about Harish. Kamlesh was shocked to learn about Harish as her parents had not told her anything about all this but Bipasha assured her that Arora uncle had settled everything, that Harish was presently assisting Arora uncle in his business and uncle was happy with his progress.

The stay for four days in New Jersey rejuvenated Kamlesh to a great extent, it sort of reconnected her with her past life. Her anger toward her parents also diminished to a large extent with the realization that her mother had to sell off her boutique and his father had to shell out a huge sum of money to save Harish and to f ght her case in the court. Both Nilanjana and Sushovan pressed her to keep in touch with them and were very happy to know that she had been admitted in graduate school. Both of them escorted her to the bus station where she boarded the bus to Syracuse on Sunday and it gave her a lot of emotional support to realize that in them she had found a well-wisher in this foreign country.

-35-

Harish was now regularly sitting in the off ce of his father and was understanding the business. He had also realised by now that all avenues of employment were closed to him and so had mellowed down considerably. He was learning the business fast, was showing interest in the work and that made his father happy. Arora was a very much changed man now. He had been deeply affected by the duel tragedy of his children and had understood that money alone could not buy you all the happiness, you have to have God's blessings also for misfortunes not to cross your path. Both Poonam and Arora were now regularly going to the Gurdwara in GK-II. He seemed very repentant in the morning, while returning from the laughter club and told Santanu "you see, I have failed in my duties as a father toward my children. I especially feel very guilty about the marriage of Kamlesh, it was me who had been fooled by the glamour of NRI and pomp and show of Prem."

Santanu said "Aroraji, anyway, whatever had to happen has happened. At least thank God that she has been saved from the clutches of that swindler".

"But her troubles are not over. My daughter is now forced to babysit and wash dishes to earn her livelihood. I had begged her not to do those things and had promised to send her money for as long as she wanted to stay there but she has refused to take any monetary help from me. I know she has not been able to pardon her father for causing her the misfortune" Arora was almost in tears.

Santanu consoled him "Please do not look at it this way. You should be thankful to the God that she is now in the company of university students of her age and has got admission in the graduate studies programme with a scholarship, all by her efforts and merit. Very few girls in her circumstances will have the guts in them to tide over the misfortune within such a short time. God's blessings are sure with her and you should be glad that she is getting back to the university once again, instead of cursing her fate doing nothing."

Arora touched his forehead with folded hands "Wahe Guru! Please make my daughter happy! She had to suffer so much misfortune at her young age, all due to my folly."

Santanu asked him "how is Harish doing in his new assignment?"

"Well, I am glad that he is taking interest and is learning fast. However, this time I have become wiser and am not spoiling him by giving him more money. I am giving him only limited pocket expenses and we have made a deal that he has to earn his share of prof ts."

Santanu said "I am sure, under your watchful eyes, he will pick up the f ner points soon and when that happens you can slowly handover major part of your business to him. Arora brightened up "I also wish the same but let us wait and watch how Harish fares."

Marriage of Anupam had been f xed and Manish received his mother's letter after coming back to New York from his trip to the Arab world. His mother wanted him to arrange his leave accordingly and come home during May. She also wanted him to f nally return to India but he knew that was not going to happen. He decided to attend his younger brother's marriage and wrote back his mother accordingly.

Agrawal had been devastated by the loss of his wife. The void created by the loss of wife of forty-f ve years of togetherness was very diff cult to come to terms with. The long-married life of togetherness had made the image of home synonymous with the wife; without Nandini, the home had lost all charm, it did not seem to have any meaning. The emptiness made him feel very lonely, he had never felt so lonely in his life, especially the long nights seemed to become unbearable. He could not sleep night after nights. He had been a constant and helpless witness to the suffering of his wife during her last days, her moaning and her contorted face due to the constant pain remained very vivid and reverberated in his mind. Why should God inf ict so much suffering to some people? Why could the end not be made quicker? and why could the terminally ill old people not be allowed some degree of dignity in their death at least during the last days? He had no answers to these questions. Doctors had turned down her repeated appeals for mercy killing saying it was against the law. But euthanasia was the only way out in such cases, bringing relief not only to the patient but to the entire family and well-wishers. If so, in the eyes of God, had he sinned? Reema telephoned her father to come and stay with them for some time in Jammu. His son-in-law Amreesh also requested him to come for a much-needed change and Agrawal decided to go to them.

Dr. Bist was offered a contract appointment of lecturer in the department for a year, which, however, was likely to continue till the vacancies were f lled and that made Bipasha very happy. Anshuman also did not want to wait any longer and so Bipasha decided to introduce him to her parents, brought him home one evening and introduced him to her parents "Ma, this is Dr. Anshuman Bist, lecturer in our deptt., about whom I have already told you."

Santanu requested him to sit down and they started talking.

Indrani asked Bipasha to prepare tea and asked him about his family.

"Aunty, my father has retired from the State Electricity Board two years back and is now settled in Dehradun. We are from Chamba in Garhwal. I have two sisters, both elder to me and married. I am the youngest.

Santanu asked "Dr. Bist, what do you want to do in life I mean regarding the choice of profession?"

Dr. Bist replied "Uncle, I wish to settle down in a university teaching job and thus pursue the academic line".

Bipasha came back with tea and snacks and all of them had tea together. Bipasha then looked at him questioningly, he hesitated and then spoke "Uncle, if you approve, I want to marry your daughter. She is ready for it" and looked at Bipasha.

Santanu looked at his daughter who said, "Well! I also want it that way if you give the consent".

Santanu looked at Indrani and then said "Well! Dr. Bist, I suggest you give us some time to think. We would let you know to say in three days. I hope you won't mind waiting for three more days." Dr. Bist agreed and left. After his departure, Indrani asked Bipasha "how much more time you would take to complete your Ph.D.?"

"My course work will be over this semester and Dr. Bist feels, it should take another two years at the max". Santanu asked, "would you like to wait that long to get married?"

"Anshuman feels we should get married this summer and then start living together. He has already moved out to rented accommodation in nearby Model Town area" Bipasha replied. Indrani reminded. "He is a north Indian from Thakur community, is from the hills, his language, food habits, way of life etc. is different from you. You will have to do a lot of adjustments. Are you prepared for that?"

"Well, he has started taking nonveg. foods while staying in a university hostel and loves Bengali foods. We have discussed the language and other differences but since we would live separately from his family, he feels those things would not present any problems."

Santanu asked, "what you would like to do after your Ph.D.?"

"Well, I also would like to settle down in the academic f eld".

Santanu thought for a while and then said as an afterthought. "It would perhaps be more appropriate if we invite him for lunch on Sunday and then communicate our decision."

Bipasha agreed immediately and hugged her father and Indrani asked her to invite Anshuman for lunch on their behalf."

Anupam's marriage had been arranged through the matrimonial columns of Hindustan Times. The girl Neha Kapoor was a teacher in Sarojini Nagar Government Girl's school. Anupam informed Manish about the date in the last week of May and asked him to come about a week earlier. He also informed his sister Raashi in Arizona and asked her to tell jijaji to arrange to leave accordingly. The reception was to be arranged in a banquet hall at the backside of the temple in GK-II and Manish asked his brother to pay the advance and book the hall well in time. There was a delicate problem also as Manish did not want to stay at home because of his restrictions and so asked for three rooms to be booked in the nearby guest house in GK-II, which was at walking distance from Himadri Apt. two for his sister and one for himself. He had to take a lot of medicines daily and did not want to let other people know about it. Similarly, brisk morning walk daily was also his necessity which he felt was to be possible if only he stayed alone.

Anupam informed that mother was quite happy with that arrangement as during the last visit of Raashi and her family, she had found to her discomfort that the children of Raashi, as well as Arjun, were very fussy about the poor sanitation and cleanliness facilities in Indian houses. Rest of the outstation relatives were to be accommodated in their own f at and one ground f oor three-bedroomed f at of their block which was lying vacant for last two years as its owner who now lived in Mumbai and did not want to give it on rent. He had agreed to give the f at to Pasricha's for a week on condition that it would be returned in spic and span condition including repairs also if there was any damage during use. Daily food requirements for the entire guests & family had been arranged in the ground f oor f at for which a good cook and two daily helps had already been booked. In all, about f fty to sixty outstation relatives were expected to stay for four to f ve days.

Manish had now become the companion of Simon and they were often seen together in Brooklyn bar. Simon by now was realizing that running a restaurant was not his cup of tea and he started leaving it more and more to his younger brother Henk. Henk was already married and his wife also was assisting him in running the restaurant. Simon started looking for a job and ultimately found one in the editorial section of the publisher of a magazine in upper Manhattan. Manish was also not pulling on well with his boss and so started thinking in terms of quitting his job in Wall Street after coming back from India. However, when he asked for leave for going to India, his leave was not granted, the plea of his boss being that just a few months back he had already taken leave for more than a month. Consequently, he had to quit his job to go to Delhi. The marriage turned out to be a grand affair. Both Raashi and Arjun were very happy with the arrangement of their stay. Manish had already arranged for the honeymoon trip of the newlyweds. All the relations were very happy to see Raashi and Manish. The marriage went off well and Manish came back to New York after Neha and Anupam left for Ooty.

On return to New York Manish felt like he had reached home. Yes! he belonged to New York now, this was the centre of his universe. His brownstone house, Basket Ball Court, Central Park, Brooklyn Bar, his friend circle all had become a part of him and he missed them while he was away. He understood the meaning of the adage-home is where your heart is, he started applying for jobs. He had prof ciency in graphic arts and he knew he was good at it. Within a month he got a good job at Sesame street, a T.V. show for children. Unlike Robert earlier and Simon now, he did not go out of the way to advertise his sexuality. He maintained discretion to avoid society's prejudices. Part of the reason also was that he had applied for US citizenship which was in process and he did not want to spoil his chances. Within a few months, his application was cleared and he became a bonaf de US citizen.

Pierre, one of the ex-companions of Simon was in great f nancial diff culty. He had lost a huge amount in the stock market and the brokers were pressing for immediate payment within a month or face impeachment. He was looking for a buyer for a two-roomed apartment that he had in Paris but was not f nding any interested party. He told Manish while in the Brooklyn Bar about his troubles and somehow got him interested in the deal. For Manish, he made a further discount and in a desperate condition became ready to transfer the ownership at a throwaway price in cash. Manish had about 80% money, rest 20% he took as a loan from his brother-in-law Arjun and bought the property through a property agent in Paris, all in a legal and transparent transaction. He had now a foothold in Europe, a place to stay in the French capital.

Simon was having problems with the police again. The urge of the authorities to 'Control Crime' had almost taken the dimensions of a fascist police state, he felt, which was alienating him, more and more from New York. There were Police checks all the time, so much so that it had grown to a proportion of abuse of civil liberties. Since he lived in a black majority area of Brooklyn and had many black friends, he was a suspect in the eyes of law. His black friends were shadowed, his car would often be stopped and thoroughly checked, some times police would come to his apartment at odd hours. Simon was very agitated when he met Manish at his house on the weekend and fumed "last week's incidents did cross all the limits."

Manish asked, "what happened?"

"I was reading Jane Eyre on a rock at the Harlem end of Central Park when suddenly a policeman appeared and accused me of drinking in public."

Manish protested "But you don't drink at all, whether in public or in private". Simon indignantly said, "I also told the same thing but they won't listen and they forced me to leave the place".

He was so much upset by these incidents that he started harbouring the wish of leaving New York for a year or two to avoid the fascist NYPD, but his problem was where to go.

Manish thought for a while and then said "Do you remember

Pierre, your ex-companion?"

"Yes! I remember, so what of him?" "Well, last year he was in great f nancial diff culty and he urgently needed to clear his substantial debts. He wanted to sell his small apartment in Paris and I bought it. That apartment is now mine and is lying vacant. If you want, you could use it as your base in Europe, in case you wanted to leave New York."

Simon, after some enquiries, liked the idea. It was settled that he would leave in a fortnight for a year or so for Paris and started making plans accordingly. Manish told him." I would meet you in Paris during X-mas holidays and we would travel across Europe if you so like" Simon was very happy and said, "I would look forward to it." He left in July for Paris.

-36-

Sushovan disposed his 'beetle' and purchased a two-year-old Pontiac car which was in a very good condition. He wanted to make a long trip and they decided to go to the Niagara falls during the long weekend of US. Independence Day in July. He wanted to see the falls from the Canadian side from where the full horseshoe-shaped falls could be seen. For this they had to go via Syracuse and Nilanjana wanted to pick up Kamlesh also. She telephoned her and f xed the programme. Both Mrinalini and Sunita were away on vacation, one to her sister in Edmonton, Canada and the other to Boston to Shabana. Kamlesh suggested," you spend the night at my place and then we would start early next morning for Niagara." Sushovan liked the idea and decided accordingly.

Dr. Gautam Tripathi's younger brother Dr. Saurav Tripathi had come to visit them in New Jersey during his summer holidays, he was doing his F.R.C.S. in Neurosurgery in Boston Medical School. Dr. Gautam wanted Sushovan to take Saurav also along with them to show the Niagara falls and he agreed. On the eve of the long weekend, Sushovan and Nilanjana picked up Dr. Saurav from his place and started early by four in the evening to avoid the long weekend heavy traff c and reached Syracuse by dusk. Nilanjana introduced Dr. Saurav to Kamlesh who had already met Dr. Gautam and Suman. She had cooked for all and they had dinner together. Dr. Saurav turned out to be a very witty and amiable person and Kamlesh had a favourable f rst impression of him.

They started early, the next morning after breakfast. Nilanjana wanted to see the scenic beauty of the Thousand Island region again and so they took the Interstate 81 to reach the Thousand Island bridge a little before the midday. The scene was breathtaking. In summer the trees were in full bloom with lush greenery spread all around. It was very diff cult for anyone not to be awed by the sheer Charm of the huge water body of the listlessly f owing St. Lawrence river meandering through the innumerable small, medium and big islands and the pure lush green environment of the wide canvas of the landscape stretching up to the distance on either side of the bridge. Dr. Saurav exclaimed "Nature in its pristine beauty! Wow! what a scene!!"

All of them got down from the car to imbibe the nature for a while, inhaling the pure air all around. Dr. Saurav took a few snaps and started small talks with Kamlesh. After working for a year in England he had emigrated to Canada, worked for a year in a hospital in Ottawa and then got admission for F.R.C.S. in Boston Medical School where he was for the last six months.

Nilanjana asked "how much time it would take to complete your FRCS?"

"It should take around three to four years". Sushovan asked "and after that?"

Dr. Saurav replied "I would like to work in some good hospitals in America and beyond that, I would think when I reach there".

He asked Kamlesh "I understand that you would be joining graduate studies starting next fall?"

She countered "How do you know?"

"Well! it has been f ashed all over the newspapers in New Jersey" he said expansively.

His response made everybody laugh. Kamlesh answered his question "yes, I will be doing my masters in Zoology". "Why Zoology?"

"Because that was what I was studying in Delhi University."

Dr.Saurav persisted "but then why didn't you complete your masters there?" he looked at her.

Kamlesh stiffened, moved away from there to cut off the conversation and leaned against the railings of the bridge as if absorbed in viewing the scenery.

Sushovan, sensing the tenseness in the situation, asked everybody to get back inside the car and they resumed the journey. Nilanjana and

Kamlesh were sitting in the back, Nilanjana attempted several times to draw Kamlesh into small talks but she remained silent. They had now entered Canada and were heading for Kingston about eighty miles from there. They reached Toronto by noon, had their lunch and then started for Niagara Falls, seventy-four miles away, reached there by around four in the afternoon and checked in the hotel rooms, booked in advance. After freshening up they left the hotel to see the Niagara falls. It was cloudy and drizzling. The famous horseshoe-shaped huge falls were hardly two km away. They parked the car at some distance, the roar of the huge body of water 2.4 million litres per second, falling two hundred feet below was like a constant din audible from a distance.

As they went near they met a thick crowd of visitors; inching forward they ultimately reached near the railings to have a full view. It was magnif cent. The water was falling, in the form of a huge horseshoe about f ve hundred metres wide, to a depth of two hundred feet with a deafening sound and raising a thick white mist rising from the depths. Down below could be seen a tranquil river carrying this enormous volume of water and ultimately Pouring it into lake Erie.

Kamlesh was overawed to witness the vast nature in its full glory, and feel its brute force and kept looking at it, forgetting the whole surrounding which roughly was the effect on all the visitors who kept clicking their cameras and videos. She did not notice when darkness had crept in and her clothes had become wet with the drizzle and mist. Suddenly the lights were switched on and another view of the falls could be seen under the powerful multicoloured light. The effect was enchanting and you could go on watching it for hours.

Dr. Saurav located her and came near, exclaiming "Fantastic! I have never witnessed anything like this before!! Nature in its full glory!!!". Kamlesh came back into the present and together they went in search of the other two. Nilanjana and Sushovan were located some distance away and Dr. Saurav bought big ice cream cones for everybody. They were all feeling chilly because of the wet clothes and so returned to the hotel, had dinner and retired for the night—ladies in one room and gents in the other. Next morning it was a bright sunny day. Kamlesh had cheered up by now and was participating in the normal way in the conversations. They went again to see the falls in bright sunlight.

They started for the return journey after lunch. Dr. Saurav offered to drive and Sushovan gladly handed over the wheels to him. They reached Syracuse by six in the evening. Kamlesh thanked Sushovan for the wonderful trip and was just getting down when Nilanjana invited her to spend the Sunday with them and Kamlesh agreed. They reached New Jersey after dark and dropped Dr. Saurav at Dr. Gautam's house when Suman invited them for lunch the next day.

In spite of much coaxing by Nilanjana, Kamlesh did not go to the Tripathi's on Sunday. Deep in her heart, she had a feeling of guilt that she did not belong to the social circle of happy people. Moreover, Dr.Saurav was paying too much attention to her and she thought it prudent to avoid his company because, by instinct, she had developed a basic distrust of men. Moreover, her past was very murky, she was neither a married nor an unmarried woman but an abandoned mistress at best. So she thought it better to avoid the company of young men, feigned a headache, begged them to excuse her and they left asking her to take rest. They thought may be it was fatigue due to the journey.

Within half an hour Dr. Saurav arrived, concern written on his face, examined her, took her Blood pressure, felt her pulse and heartbeat. Everything seemed normal. Puzzled, he looked at her penetratingly. Unable to bear his look, she asked, "so, what is the diagnosis?"

"Very alarming! that you want to avoid my company, but the question is why?" he told in all seriousness.

His tone was such that Kamlesh had to smile "but I thought that you were a Surgeon and not a psychologist?" "Well, whatever! but my bhabhi has given me strict instructions to fetch you and I can't disappoint the whole household" he looked at her.

"So, it seems I have no option but to go."

"Exactly, that was the consensus at the other end also."

While driving, Dr. Saurav asked her "can I give you a small suggestion both as a friend as well as a doctor?" She looked at him "yes and what?"

"You tend to cut yourself off from time to time; it encourages depressing thoughts, shunning positive thinking. So please take things easy, at your age you should not be so serious."

Kamlesh did not say anything.

Everybody was very happy to see Kamlesh and welcomed her. Mrs. Tripathi who was only a few years older to her pressed her hands and apologetically said "it was my fault that last night I did not invite you separately, I hope you did not mind. Here we are quite informal with each other, so please join us, "and asked her to sit by her side, with her three-year-old son Abhishck sitting on her lap.

Dr. Gautam was narrating an interesting episode from his school days. "I was a student may be of class seven or eight in S.S.D. School in Meerut at that time. We had a very strict English teacher, who had a bad habit of brushing up the lesson taught on the previous day including the diff cult spellings of that lesson before starting the new chapter. We were studying in a boys school and his rule was that anybody not answering correctly, would receive a punishment of f ve lashes from a cane. It was the job of the class monitor to arrange, daily, a robust-looking green cane, placed neatly on his table before he arrived in the class.

Suman asked "why green? was that his favourite colour?"

"No, because the greenness of the twig ensured that it was very f exible and the lashing with it produced the effect of a whip, its instant effect being the victim crying with pain, which gave a sadistic pleasure to the teacher".

Nilanjana disgustingly asked, "and the parents did not object to this kind of corporal punishments?"

"No, fortunately, or unfortunately, the parents in those days and in that region, also believed in the same policy. 'Spare the rod and spoil the child' especially the male child and he had the reputation of being a good teacher."

Saurav asked, "anyway, so what happened to your story?"

"Oh yes! for the last few days at that time, our uncle with his whole family had come to us and I was so busy in playing with the cousins that I had totally forgotten about the English class," he looked around for better effect and then resumed "my usual seat was the f rst one on the f rst bench in the second row from the left; the last boy in the f rst row on the right was being grilled and I was waiting for my turn next, with a palpitating heart. Just then, as if like a God sent, the peon came with a circular and the teacher read it loudly for the whole class. While he was doing so, I slipped quietly from my seat and sat on the last row f rst from the left, quite satisf ed that I was saved by the grace of God."

Sushovan protested "that was cheating." Dr. Gautam nodded "God also must have thought so because, in the distraction of reading the circular, the teacher forgot whose turn it was next. He remained undecided for a moment, then made up his mind and shouted "O.K., you on the last row from the left, stand up please", he gestured with his cane.

"I stood up like a puppet. But the moment he saw my face, he recognized me and roared "you were sitting on the second row, how did you go there? I mumbled something but he did not care to listen. He asked me two spellings and I could not answer correctly. Unfortunately on that particular day, all the f rst row students had answered correctly and the cane had not yet been tested. He gestured with his cane, asking me to come to his table. I went there like a lamb just to be slaughtered but took care not to come within the striking distance of the cane. He noted this and beckoned me in a very sweet inviting tone "come nearer". I inched forward. He asked in a very calm voice. "Now stretch your right palm." The moment I did so, he lashed his cane three times with all the vengeance. Writhing from the pain, I shrank back. He roared "Stretch your left hand," I obeyed and immediately received two more full blows" Dr.Gautam looked around "the terror written on my face and tears in my eyes satisf ed him that the treatment was having the desired effect, but he was not still fully satisf ed. "This is for the wrong spellings and now for the cheating part! Come nearer" and I went nearer like a hypnotized lamb. This time, with the precision of an expert hunter, he lashed thrice on my buttocks. I was still smarting with pain and humiliation when the bell rang to the relief of everybody except the teacher and he left the class." Everybody was doubling up with guffaws of laughter and even Kamlesh smiled.

Sushovan now narrated his ordeal. "I also must have been of the same age at that time and was the cricket captain of my team in Burdwan. We had a great rivalry with a nearby locality and their captain sent us a letter challenging our cricket skills on the f eld of the park, for a game on the next Sunday and we accepted the challenge.

Somehow due to great publicity by words of mouth, its importance was greatly hyped and on Sunday a sizable crowd assembled on the ground. We played f rst followed by them and due mainly to the batting prowess of their captain Nimai, they eventually defeated us". He looked around and continued "What happened next was very sad. Amidst all the booings, catcalls and jeering, Nimai suddenly asked his boys to catch hold of me, the captain of the rival team. I was forced to bend forward and then he poked the pointed end of the wicket in my arse. I cried out loud, not due to pain but more due to the public humiliation. The onlookers cheered them on and clapped vigorously at my plight, I realised that the mob only adores the winners. Not only they snatched my bat but painted my face black also. All my teammates had run away by then and I had to come back alone crying all the way."

Again, there was a huge round of laughter. It seemed Suman and Nilanjana were especially delighted with the ordeals of their husbands and were bursting with peels of laughter coming in waves. Dr. Gautam as if to neutralise them, innocently asked: "Suman, you have such a good voice, why don't you sing a song so that we also could enjoy?"

This caught her off guard "Me? no, no, I am not a singer and it is getting late for lunch." She stood up and hurried to the kitchen.

Nilanjana looked at Kamlesh "Bipasha told me you are a good singer. Why don't you sing a song for us?" and everybody looked at her. Before Kamlesh could say anything Dr. Saurav stood up, asked everybody to be silent and announced." So here goes the best item of the day" and gestured her to begin.

Kamlesh shyly sang a Lata Mangeshkar hit. Towards the end Suman came out of the kitchen and said "please sing another one as I could not properly hear your f rst song" and Kamlesh sang another one but then burst into tears. Everybody became very much concerned, Nilanjana and Suman ran to her but she composed herself immediately. "I suddenly remembered my home, I am missing it so much", to the relief of everyone. They broke for lunch.

Dr. Saurav complimented her for the good voice and she replied: "I am singing after almost a year, for the f rst time since coming to USA and thank you for coaxing me to come over here". Dr. Saurav was f attered "That means you are not angry with me any more, but please tell me, what prevented you from singing for such a long time?" and looked at her.

Kamlesh again went into her shell, did not reply and moved away. After lunch, Sushovan and Nilanjana left and dropped Kamlesh to the bus station for boarding a bus to Syracuse.

Next day, after Sushovan had gone to the lab, Suman and Dr. Saurav dropped in at Nilanjana's on their way to 'Safeway' for groceries. Dr. Saurav was getting very curious to know about the mood swings of Kamlesh and asked Nilanjana straightway "there is something abnormal about Kamlesh, she looks a troubled girl somewhere. The moment you ask about her past, she coils into her shell, the same thing happened yesterday as well as in the Niagara falls also. She seems to have some mental block somewhere" he enquiringly looked at her.

Nilanjana hesitated for a few moments and then decided to tell the truth "there has been a great tragedy in her life, she is still desperately trying to come out of it and it has taken its emotional toll", she told them the entire story.

Both of them listened to it very attentively and Dr. Saurav exclaimed "Oh! What a nerve of steel to face it alone in a foreign country". Nilanjana continued "she comes from a rich family but she has decided to face her troubles alone by declining any monetary support from her parents. She is maintaining herself by doing babysitting and dishwashing jobs and has already cleared the exams to secure admission in graduate school with scholarship starting this September. She has decided to do her Ph.D. f rst and be f nancially independent before she decides about her future".

Suman said, "may God help her in achieving her goals".

Nilanjana cautioned "she will be very angry if she knows that I have told you about her. She hates being pitied for her misfortune".

Dr. Saurav asked, "How did you know all these details?"

"My husband's niece back home is her closest friend and a friend of mine also, she has told us and through her introduction only, we have met Kamlesh," Dr. Saurav said "I didn't know that Indian girls also possessed such grit and determination to f ght the odds. She does not know that she is going to become a role model of future if she can shape up her own destiny."

Suman pressed the hands of Nilanjana "please call her again during X-mas holidays. We would like to meet her again"

Saurav commented, "she seems a real-life heroine, straight out of an American bestseller f ction, dumped by fate into a dustbin and crawling out of it......."

<h1 style="text-align:center">-37-</h1>

Agrawal had come back from Reema's house after two months and was very rejuvenated. He made it a point to keep his lifestyle simple from here on. He sold his car as he felt he did not much need it. He donated his computer along with the table to the RWA off ce, large fridge to the co-operative stores, keeping only the smaller one with him. He asked his daughters to come and take away the jewellery, clothing and other valuables of their late mother and then donated the remaining part. This emptied the house quite a bit. After the death of Nandini, he felt less and less attached to the worldly goods and comforts. He started cooking his food to keep him busy. RWA elections were coming and he was persuaded to become the President. The new team had Nair as vice President, Santanu as secretary, Kaul as security in-charge and Subramaniam as treasurer. The entries of the account were now kept in the computer f les, and RWA work kept Agrawal busy. His other jobs being treasurer of the co-op stores and secretary of the laughter club.

Pahuja had retired from Lucknow and had come back to Delhi. He was now a very obese person about twenty kgs overweight. His son and daughter both were in England, gainfully employed and Pahujas also was going to England in the Summer for a few months. Pahuja had rejoined the laughter club, which now had many new faces. Several old members had either died or had moved away with their children in other cities or abroad. Subhash Dhingra, who was the host for the day asked Agrawal "how do you manage to be the off ce bearers of so many organizations? "I am secretary of S-Block, G.K.-II and that takes away all my time and also brings me into conf ict with vested interest groups or individuals, raising my blood pressure unnecessarily". Agrawal replied "It happened with me also initially. In time I got associated with other organizations also, simultaneously managing several posts and then learnt the trade secret only by experience".

Others also started getting interested and converged to listen better. Bhatia from Neelachal shouted, "Boss, share the secret with us also".

"Well! my experience over the years has taught me two things and you have to remember these two basic points: the f rst one is that all these social works are thankless jobs, so don't get too much involved. Try to go with the majority view as far as possible." Dr. Sharma from Gangotri asked," and the second one?"

"The second point and I follow it as a cardinal rule that don't stick to a post for too long. Just come out of it after one or two terms."

Dhingra, who was into his third term, asked: "why?"

"Because the longer you hold your off ce, you realize you will make more enemies, will be criticized for your errors and omissions. So quit before it generates bad blood. It is not worth, let somebody else handle it."

Pahuja interrupted "you say, don't get involved, but how can you avoid that?"

"See, you have to keep in mind that the organization was running before you joined it and would keep running even after you are gone. However, I would say that better don't put all your energies on one post, take another post elsewhere in which you will f nd an alternative outlet to do something for the society and so the net result would be that your involvement would be divided."

Dr. Sharma, who was the president of Gangotri apartment enquired "why don't you come and give a talk in our M.C. where the members are constantly f ghting with each other?"

Agrawal Shrugged" if you wish, I am ready" and they dispersed.

Partho was being sent to USA by his employers on a three-year posting. He had come home from Bangalore, on a leave for two weeks before leaving for Atlanta in three months. Santanu with his family decided to make a trip to Hardwar by his car, primarily to meet Bipasha's would-be in-laws in Dehradun. They stayed in a hotel in Hardwar and went to Dehradun next day. Anshuman welcomed them in his house and introduced them to his parents. Mr. Bist was older than Santanu, they were simple people, had a modest house built more than ten years ago during his last posting in Dehradun. Mrs. Bist called Bipasha inside to help her in the kitchen, while Anshuman and parents kept talking to each other. Mr. Bist told "we are Garhwaisl from the hills and hail from Chamba but life in the hills, especially in the old age, is diff cult so we decided to settle here.

Santanu asked, "Do you still have any connection with the hills?"

"Yes, yes, we have our ancestral house with some land, looked after by my younger brother. We go there every summer for a few weeks."

In the meantime, Bipasha brought tea etc and they had tea together. Partho had not met Anshuman earlier and they started talking and went out. Mrs. Bist had some arthritic problem and was slow in her movements. After some hesitation, she asked," Please don't feel offended but we are a bit scared of the Delhiwallahs".

Indrani asked, "why?"

She looked at her husband and told: "they are not honest and very manipulative is a general feeling."

Indrani felt embarrassed but Santanu laughed heartily and said: "you are perhaps right but let me assure you we are Bengalees and from Kolkata, we are in Delhi in connection with the job only."

Mr. Bist asked, " Do you plan to settle down there?"

"I have purchased a f at and presently am staying there, most likely we will settle down in Delhi."

Mrs. Bist asked, "Do you still have any connection with Kolkata?" Indrani replied "yes, his, as well as my parents, are still living there, we have our ancestral house and keep going there".

Mr. Bist said "look, Paharis are simple and honest people. We do not also have the glamorous lifestyle of Delhi. Moreover, it is going to be an intercaste marriage between a Brahmin and a Thakur, do you think it will work out?" Santanu answered "that is what I also had asked my daughter but she feels it should not present many problems. I feel it would be better if you call your son here, let Bipasha and your son answer the question and let us see what they have to say?

Mrs. Bist called her son, both Partho and Anshuman entered, sat in the room and Mr. Bist posed the question to him. Anshuman replied. "We both have discussed this aspect in detail and feel we can overcome the differences." Mrs. Bist now asked Bipasha" Beti, as a wife you have to adapt yourself more to our way of life as that is the expectation of the society. I can tell you that such adjustments may not be very easy and would also test your patience. Are you prepared for all that?" Bipasha replied "I know but I feel in all the marriages such adjustment problems come. Only in my case, it will be slightly more". She looked at Anshuman and said, "with his co-operation, we feel, we will overcome the hurdles."

Both Mr. Bist and Santanu agreed "Well! as parents, we want to see our children happy and settled in life and their happiness is our happiness."

Indrani now asked "my son is going to USA in three months, we would very much like if the marriage can be solemnized before that so that he also can be a part of it. What do you say?"

Mrs. Bist looked at her husband, who looked at Anshuman and then asked Santanu "we were not prepared for the date, would you please allow us for a little private consultation?"

Both Indrani and Santanu said "by all means. You take your own time and could let us know even after a few days" and the Bists went to the other room.

After a while, Mr. Bist came out. We do not have any problems as such but I will have to consult my elders and then would let you know after a few days."

Santanu said "No problem, let Anshuman convey your decision to us in Delhi" and then as an afterthought added" in that case, we would then suggest you a few dates, after consulting our priest and after mutual agreement would f nalise the date. The marriage would be in Delhi and in traditional Bengali tradition and we will make all arrangements for your board and lodge there, after hearing from you the number of Baratis from outstation".

Mr. Bist agreed "We would let you know that also through Anshu" From Dehradun Santanu went to the hill station Mussorie to spend a day there. Indrani asked Bipasha on the way "now that the things have been f nalized, you have to go in that family."

Bipasha asked, "how do you f nd them?" Santanu said "I liked the family, they are simple people".

Partho added "Dr. Anshuman seems to be a nice chap. Didi your selection is O.K. It would be very nice if the marriage is solemnized before I leave."

Kaul had retired from his bank and soon enough he got a job at Modi Towers in Nehru Place. Sukriti was continuing in the Army Public School but the commuting each way was taking about one and a half hour due to increased traff c. She was thinking of taking voluntary retirement as soon as Shweta, their only daughter f nished her studies. Shweta had grown into a beautiful woman and was now in the f rst year of M.B.A. from Delhi University's Faculty of Management Studies. (F.M.S). Kaul and Santanu often had lunch together at Sona restaurant as Santanu was working in the nearby Vishal Bhawan. Kaul asked Santanu. "How is your daughter's wedding plans going?"

Santanu replied "Anshuman informed us last week that the date October 3 or 5 would be O.K. for them. We have now f nalized October 5 as the marriage date and have ordered the printing of invitation cards. The venue would be Chittaranjan Memorial Hall in C.R. Park and I have already booked the hall, arranged the caterer and booked two nearby guest houses in C.R. Park to accommodate the Baratis and have also booked a bus to transport them from Dehradun & back."

Kaul was relieved "so your worries are over?"

"Only thing that remains is the marketing for the marriage and distribution of the invitation cards".

Agrawal had seen an advertisement in the newspaper wherein the Govt. of Delhi had invited the RWAs and other citizen groups to participate in a new initiative of the government, the Bhagidari scheme, whereby a regular forum was to be made available to the residents as well as the govt. to hear each other directly with an emphasis on f nding solutions, thereby the government establishing a direct linkage with the citizen groups to hear their viewpoints, with an aim for good governance. Agrawal called a meeting of the M.C. and after much deliberations, the

RWA decided to join the scheme. Secretary was entrusted to prepare an application along with the necessary documents and submit it to the concerned department. Kaul complained in the meeting that he was not happy with the security guards, as they were regularly leaving the job, the agency not providing adequate replacements in time, as a result, the security was becoming lax. It was decided to change the agency and he was entrusted to collect quotations from other agencies.

Mrs. Baluja asked Garima who had now moved to their own f at at Vasant Kunj, to come and take whatever would be useful to her, so that she would dispose of the rest, rent out the f at and would move out to the 'Old Age Home' for the ladies at Patel Nagar where she had got accommodation and was now living. She used to periodically come to her f at to interview the prospective tenants and show them the f at. She was sitting with Indrani in her f at on Sunday afternoon and Indrani asked: "How is the life there?"

"It is a sort of furnished hostel life. You have your own room, with limited essential amenities, you don't have to cook and manage your household and that gives relief to people of my age. This also means you have a lot of spare time at your disposal and so has everybody who is there. We gossip, share each other's life between ourselves, do some exercise, some yoga to keep f t. The home is managed by competent people and they provide personalized care also".

Indrani asked, "How do you like the food over there?"

"Well! it is not as good as homemade food, it is also fully vegetarian and you don't have as many choices either. It is a common menu to include the tastes of all the residents. But it is hygienic and neat and clean. If you are not very fussy, it is O.K. I am satisf ed."

Indrani asked "Can you periodically go out to restaurants or order food on home delivery?"

"You can but the older inmates are not in favour, saying that the food from the market is very oily and spicy which upsets their system and so people generally avoid doing it."

Bipasha asked" aunty, do they allow you to periodically go out or allow you to meet visitors who may come to see you?"

"Yes, we have to inform the manager in advance and enter the name of the visitor in the Register or where we are going. There are specif ed time and days when visitors are allowed" Bipasha said, "aunty someday we will come there to meet you."

"You are welcome" and then Mrs. Baluja enquired Indrani "how are the marriage arrangements progressing?"

Indrani said "the invitation cards have been distributed, Mr.Agrawal has made his house available for the outstation guests from our side, the f at at the ground f oor which is locked, also has been provided by its owner for a week and with the arrangement of a cook the arrangements are complete more or less" and as an afterthought added "do you think there will be any diff culty in your coming?" "You see, I don't drive any more after dark. My ref exes are not as good as before"

"No problem, I will ask Partho to fetch you from your Home, but we all would very much like you to bless the newlyweds and be present in the ceremony."

Sukriti and Mrs. Subramanium also came to meet her. Indrani told Bipasha to tell Sukriti aunty what she had known about that Bansal boy. Bipasha informed "Sudhakar Bansal's father is a Prof. in the History dept. of D.U. and they live in Maurice Nagar. Anshuman has talked to Sudhakar's teachers in M.B.A. and they rate him as a good student".

Mrs. Baluja asked, "what is cooking, Sukriti?"

"Nothing is f nal as yet but you know Shweta is getting chummy with this fellow lately and so thought we should f nd out about his background". Mrs. Baluja approved. "It looks good, may be another union is in the making" Sukriti was not so sure "Shweta is very headstrong you know. I only hope the relationship goes to the logical conclusion and not abort in the midway."

Mrs. Subramanium asked Bipasha "So, you must be counting your days now?"

"No, aunty, I am very worried. My experimental work in the Lab is not progressing very satisfactorily and is not anywhere near completion and I fear my Ph.D. might get further delayed, "she seemed very concerned. All the ladies laughed loudly at this. Mrs. Baluja said, "marriage is not dependent on whether you are a Ph.D. or not and Ph.D. can wait."

Arora was not the spirited happy go lucky type any more. The twin tragedy of his children had left a deep scar in his mind, both he and Poonam had lately become quite religious also. Probably, when nothing works in your life, you take solace in the Shelter of God in search of some emotional strength to face the odds.

While coming back from the laughter Club Agrawal commented "Aroraji, you seem to be very serious now. What happened to your earlier joyful spirit?"

"See! earlier I was under the false impression that I can buy all happiness in life with money but the events of Kamlesh and Harish have taught me that money can buy you only a limited comfort-related happiness but you need to have God's blessings, in addition, to be happy in your life which does not depend on your money power somehow."

Agrawal sighed "you don't have to convince me about that, I have lately gone through that painful realization myself" and they kept walking silently.

Indrani phoned Sushovan and Nilanjana, informed them of the marriage date and they promised to come well in time. Altogether about f fty outstation guests, both from Santanu and her side were to be accommodated and arrangements had been made accordingly for about a week.

Himadri RWA had been enlisted in the Bhagidari scheme and had been invited to a meeting with the high govt. off cials of various departments and chaired by the chief minister, to be held at Pragati Maidan next week. Agrawal, Santanu and Kaul were to represent their RWA. Security passes were issued for them and all the delegates took their seats in the big hall, with the Chief Minister and off cials from various wings of the government, sitting on the dais. The chief minister inaugurated the meeting citing the purpose of Bhagidari was to have direct contact between the residents and the service providers and also highlighted the achievements of the govt. Chief Secretary elucidated the purpose of the interaction with the resident groups was to get direct feedback from them about their problems and aspirations for speedy redressals of their needs. The meeting went off well.

Sushovan and Nilanjana arrived three days before the marriage. They were to spend the night at Lopamudra's house whereas during the day they were to be with Indrani. The marriage ceremony turned out to be a grand affair. The whole contingent from Rajagiri school including the principal Father Thomas and Vice-Principal Father John were there as were the friend circles of Santanu, Partho, Bipasha as well as the local and outstation relatives. The Baratis had been well-taken care off, Partho had brought Mrs. Baluja also. Indrani, in between, introduced Sushovan to Poonam "meet my brother, whose marriage you had attended last year. He now lives in New Jersey."

Poonam's face radiated "yes! Yes!! Bipasha told me that you have met my daughter Kamlesh who now lives at Syracuse".

Sushovan replied "yes auntie, we know her well, she has stayed with us also" and he called his wife to meet her.

Poonam pressed Nilanjana's hands "she does not keep much contact with us any more, must be very angry with us for spoiling her life.... Nilanjana took her aside and consoled her "please don't get so upset, her worst is over and she is trying hard to come out of the trauma."

Poonam pressed her hands "you don't know how great a favour you have done to us by providing her with the support when she needed it most, please come to our house before you leave"

Sushovan said, "O.K. after the Baratis leave by afternoon tomorrow, we will come to your house in the evening."

Sushovan and Nilanjana reached Arora's house next evening and showed them the photos at Niagara Falls and at New Jersey with Kamlesh and the whole family saw them all with full attention. Arora told them with all humility "It was all my folly but I could never imagine that an NRI can be such a crook."

Sushovan consoled him "your daughter is very courageous, she is trying hard to establish her own identity and someday you will see her rise to the top."By now Poonam also had joined him. Arora said. "We have not done anything for her, Kamlesh deserves all the kudos for bringing back her life on the right track" and then as an afterthought added, "please take it from this old man that don't run after money and glamour, it is often so misleading." Sushovan gave all the photos to Aroras and came back.

Sushovan could meet his parents and the relatives in Delhi itself so did not go to Kolkata and by next evening all the relatives left the house. Santanu, Indrani, Partho, Nilanjana and Sushovan started the follow- ing morning for Dehradun by car, to attend the reception given at the end of the bridegroom.

By evening they checked in at the hotel at Dehradun, in the rooms reserved for them by Anshuman. At night they attended the reception, where Sushovan handed over to Anshuman the full hotel reservation for three days in Missouri for their honeymoon trip including local sightseeing trip. Bipasha was very happy to see them all in the reception. After reception Santanus returned to the hotel and started for Delhi the next morning. Sushovan & Nilanjana left for USA the same night, followed by Partho two days later.

-38-

Kamlesh had joined the university as a graduate student, the scholarship had eased her f nancial problems also. In the f rst semester, she had to take three credits and was happy to be a student again. Amanda had found a new baby sitter for Pamela, Amanda had thrown a small party on the occasion of the birthday of Pamela in which Kamlesh, Mrinalini and Sunita were also invited. Sunita and Mrinalini many times had asked Kamlesh to come to the get-togethers of the Indian community but she steadfastly avoided them and shunned any contacts with the local Indian community, primarily due to stigma of her past.

Simon arrived in Paris in July and went to the apartment of Manish near the Pigalle metro station to set himself there. It was a small apartment in the less prosperous section of Paris and had not been maintained well. His f rst job was to make it livable by calling the plumber, electrician and painter. After this was done and after the purchase of some new furniture, the apartment seemed O.K. and he started living there. Three girls who were sharing the same apartment were his next-door neighbours, they were all working women and could speak English which made things easier for him in the new environment. Within two months Simon picked up enough French to get along with his day to day life. One of the girls Nicole was going for grape picking for about a fortnight in the vineyards of Bordeaux and she invited Simon also to join her to get this new experience.

The grapes in France mature in August-September and that is the grape picking season for which a good number of labourers were needed. Generally, students earned some extra money by doing this and farmers usually sent their requirements to the student's off ce in the universities which was then displayed on the notice boards. The students then made direct contacts with the farmers concerned who gave them free board and lodge plus some daily allowance. Nicole had picked up the address from the notice board at Sorbonne and they proceeded for Bordeaux where they spent a fortnight picking grapes. The good thing was that at the end of two weeks in the vineyard, his French became quite f uent and he could participate in small talks also.

Nicole and Simon became good friends and primarily through her efforts, Simon got a school job of teaching English. He bought the French version of people's car Renault and started his new life in Paris as a resident.

Manish left New York during the Christmas holidays. Simon came to receive him at the Orly airport and they drove to the apartment. Both were very excited to be with each other after a long absence. For about a week they were in Paris and Simon showed him the places of tourist interests around the city including the Versailles Palace about 20 km away. Paris was a very beautiful city situated on both sides of the banks of river Seine and was full of gardens, monuments, Churches and palaces. The French way of life also seemed much relaxed as compared to the American way and Simon was enjoying the freedom he had in this country. After a week they planned to visit Spain which had a warmer climate. Simon's one colleague had suggested that if he was going south of France, he should also pay a short visit to a Gandhi Ashram "La Bori Noble" for a few days. His colleague was a regular visitor to the place for the last few years and gave Simon an introduction letter.

They started early in the morning and drove to come out of the city taking the autoroute to Orleans, continuing South via Bourz, Nevers, Leons where they stayed for the night. The terrain started becoming hilly as they reached Valance the next day. They reached Montpellier by evening and stayed for the night in a hotel. Next morning continuing further they reached a small town Lodeve before noon and took the hilly road to a small village Rockerdond on top of the hill from where the road descended and they reached a small railway station Cabril within an hour. From Cabril, the Ashram was only about, two km away and they reached 'La Bori Noble' by midday.

Simon showed the letter to the concerned person and they were ushered in the dormitory to stay for a few days. La Bori Noble was far away from the madding crowd, situated in the lap of nature in between the hilly terrain, having about a hundred residents leading a very peaceful life in a rural sort of set up completely devoid of the trappings of the urban world including electricity. It was founded by a French writer Lanza del Vasto who had been a disciple of Gandhiji in 1937 in India and had set up this place as a replica of his Ashram. Both Manish and Simon were very surprised to f nd such a place amidst the plenty of the materialistic West. The founder was now dead but the Ashram was still run on his principles.

A core group of people lived there permanently but the majority were sort of tourists who spent here from few days to few months and some were regular visitors. Mostly people came there to take a total break from the hustle and bustle of the busy urban city life and its materialistic lifestyle. Everybody had to work here which was assigned to him or her after the group prayer in the morning, followed by breakfast. The community cleared the virgin land around it, made it worthy of agriculture, ploughed and grew its own food, had its dairy, fruit and vegetable gardens, people ate simple vegetarian food, performed yoga and the day ended with sundown, by which time people f nished their dinner in the dining hall, prepared by their members and then retired to their rooms. It was mostly hard physical labour, people used to toil for the day and rested after dark. Both Manish and Simon used to have sound sleep. No drinks or smoking was permitted and people led a very austere and frugal life. After spending a happy and peaceful life there for a week, Manish and Simon started for Spain early in the morning. After enjoying the sun in Barcelona for a week, they started for the return journey, Manish and Simon taking the wheels alternately and reached Paris. The holidays for Manish was getting over and he f ew to New York the next day.

The f rst semester exams of Kamlesh were over and she had passed them with 'A' grades. She had to take another three courses in the next semester. The X-mas vacations had started and the university looked deserted. Nilanjana had telephoned her several times to spend a few days with them and see the video of Bipasha's marriage and she decided to go. Mrinalini had started writing her thesis and Sunita had also f nished her experimental work and awaiting the go-ahead from her professor to start writing her thesis. However, this meant that within six months or so both of them would go away and then she will have to f nd alternative accommodation. She decided she, in that case, would move out to a single room and do her light housekeeping and that way she would be able to concentrate on her studies. She went to see Pamela and Amanda who were going home the next day to Albany to meet her parents.

Next day Sushovan and Nilanjana picked Kamlesh up at the bus station at Hoboken and brought her home. Nilanjana posted her with the recent news of their Delhi visit including meeting the Aroras and showed her the video of Bipasha's marriage. Partho, who was now in Atlanta, had come to meet them. Kamlesh knew him well and was very happy to see him. Nilanjana conf ded to her "I am pregnant and would be going back to Delhi in a few months if in case, my mother can not come here and stay with us for a few months. Kamlesh congratulated her and Partho updated Kamlesh about his job at Atlanta and accommodation etc.

Nilanjana had invited the Tripathi's to dinner in the evening. Dr. Saurav also had come on a short leave and he was very happy to see Kamlesh and exclaimed "Well! Well!! so we meet here again and thank you for coming." Kamlesh introduced Partho to them and they shook hands. Dr Saurav said. "We are going to see the Statue of Liberty tomorrow. I say, let us all go together."

Both Nilanjana and Partho immediately gave their consent. As the statue was approachable by boat directly from New Jersey, Dr. Saurav left along with Partho right away to buy the tickets for the ferry. By the time they returned pre-dinner round of drinks were served by Sushovan and supplemented with hot pakauris brought from the kitchen by Kamlesh.

Nilanjana and Suman were preparing the snacks while Dr. Gautam was entertaining his son Abhishek who was now three and a half years old. Sushovan handed over the glasses to Dr. Saurav and Partho also and they sat together, joined in a while by ladies also.

Dr. Saurav announced "So, we start at nine-thirty sharp tomorrow morning from this house" and everybody agreed. The discussion very soon veered round an interesting topic—the world can not sustain for very long, the high level of consumerism as prevalent in USA.

Dr. Gautam said, "whatever you say, but a reversal of the process is not possible any more".

Dr. Saurav intervened "there is a way but for that to happen, the lifestyle change is a must".

Sushovan opined "with the increasing level of prosperity and urbanization, the degree of consumerism is only increasing and you can't order people suddenly to consume less".

Partho was not in favour of this, he said: "see, unless people consume more and more, the industries will not be able to survive and our prosperity is directly dependent on the degree of industrialization". Dr.Saurav interrupted" agreed, but what is the cumulative effect of the consumerist lifestyle, which translated into simpler words, can be put as – what is the environmental cost of the all-pervasive consumerism?" Suman protested" why are you so much against consumerism, you don't want to see people enjoying the comforts?" Dr. Saurav, it seemed, was waiting to hear this line of thought. He argued, "Consumerism gives rise to individualism i.e. you want to possess everything for yourself only, you are not prepared to share things with others and this is exactly the mentality which the industry wants, to sell more and more of the consumer goods."

Partho protested "but consumer goods satisfy our needs."

Dr. Saurav continued "agreed, but see, then families are not satisf ed with one car, one laptop or one mobile. Everybody wants exclusively for their use. Possessing things gives you status. You can't share your parental house, you have to have your own f at, own car and so on. Do you think all that is necessary?" Dr. Gautam chipped in "look, with increasing level of prosperity, the individualism also increases and USA is the epicentre of maximum individualism. Everybody wants more and more of everything for himself and that is in spite of the national debt which is increasing to alarming proportions."

Dr. Saurav commented "that is the point. There is overconsumption all around. People are not satisf ed with small T.V., small fridge, small car, small house, they want big and more comfort." Sushovan pointed out" True, but this is also the result of too easy consumer credits being made available by the f nancial institutions, which in other words could perhaps be more appropriately termed as immoral lending which encourages people to invest more and more into this so-called 'American dream' to have more and more even if they can not afford it". Dr. Saurav pointed out" that is exactly what I am saying. God forbid, if this hyper-consumerism bubble bursts someday, so many thousands of Americans will suddenly go broke."

Suman countered "may be what you say has some degree of truth but think—if you reject this senseless consumerism, you will no longer be considered honourable in the society. If you don't have or simply can't f aunt money, you simply don't count."

Nilanjana, who was until now listening also joined "and this is the culture which is sadly permeating in the Indian society also, especially in Delhi."

Partho chipped in "f aunt money and be counted, else you are no more a part of the current Indian dream. I have lived in Bangalore also and let me tell you, it is not any different there also. The dominant theme is to make money, by hook or by crook and then f aunt it."

Dr. Saurav agreed "and that brings us back to the original point that this society is not only living beyond its economic means but also of its environmental means. The word austerity is totally missing from the US way of life and in general from the developed world's way of life, let me tell you I have lived in UK and Canada also."

Kamlesh now chipped in "why blame the western world only, back in India also are we not blindly aping the western way of life?, in India also we want 'f ve star' culture, we want to do it with style, and go for more and more spending in our social functions in order to make it more ostentatious.

Dr. Gautam joined "how much our, I mean Indian, lifestyle has changed lately–our whole Hindu philosophy was centred around the value system of austerity in our day to day life hardly about up to one generation ago, our Rishis and saints, since ages, have commanded more respect than even the kings but alas! all those old virtues are gone, rather has been discarded. In India also, I found, our new generation worships only money and nothing else. If you can not f aunt money, you are simply not counted. Austerity has become a negative word altogether."

Suman interrupted him "wait, wait? let us f rst try to understand what does austerity mean in our modern-day context"?

Dr. Saurav tried to explain "Well! it is associated with making personal changes in your way of living which benef ts society and which makes sense to people who have learned to tackle wastefulness by cutting the consumption level."

Sushovan added "like may be, what is lately being coined as reducing our carbon foot print, then start believing in sharing things, recycling of discarded consumables, also reducing the dependence on air travels, or on taking lavish vacations or in using public transport instead of being cocooned in our big sized automobiles etc., etc."

Dr. Gautam further added "we also should start respecting the words like simplicity, thrift, sustainability etc. and not phoo-phooing and thinking them as derogatory or negative words. Instead of blaming the government for all the ills plaguing the society, are we ready to practice austerity in our personal lives? "he looked around.

Kamlesh observed "these things are easy to say but may be very diff cult to put in practice, especially if the society as a whole does not believe in these ideals. You will simply end up as a mismatch" Suman applauded "well said, I agree with you."

Nilanjana got up and silenced everybody" enough of these intellectually stimulating discussions as appetizers, let us now proceed to the dinner".

Everybody lapped up the idea. Dr. Saurav moaned "Ah! I am starving and am fully ready for a sumptuous dinner." Kamlesh remarked, "I have surveyed the kitchen but am sorry to say that I did not f nd much sign of austerity there". Sushovan exclaimed "thank God for the mercy" and joined the queue.

Next morning the Tripathi's reached a sharp nine-thirty and found Sushovan & Co. waiting for, them. They went together to the Liberty State Park Jetty and boarded the ferry starting at ten. It was a festive mood all around, being during the Christmas holidays and the boat soon reached the Liberty Island. There was no entry fee for the statue–which had been a gift from the people of France to the people of USA and was looked like a universal symbol of freedom and democracy. It was dedicated to the nation in 1886 and made a national monument in 1924. They all went to the top, went around the island leisurely and had lunch there. Post-lunch they visited Ellis Island to see the museum depicting the history of America. While seeing the museum Dr. Saurav paired up with Kamlesh. They looked together at the American history for a while and Kamlesh suddenly asked him "I hear from Suman bhabhi that you did not agree to the arranged marriage f xed by your parents and helped the girl in marrying somebody else, is that true?" and looked at him.

He shrugged "I would say both yes and no". She was perplexed

"now what is that supposed to mean? "Oh! may be I had no choice". "Why?"

"It is a long story, may be I will tell you some other time. But by the by, I have also heard about your story" and looked straight at her.

She stiffened "I have nothing to say" and went ahead. He caught her up" I have great admiration for your courage to start your life again. By the by, how are your graduate studies progressing?" "Not bad, I still have miles to go" and then asked, "how is your FRCS programme going?"

"I am still at the learning stage. They have very advanced techniques." Just then Partho spotted them from somewhere and said: "others have f nished and they are waiting for you." They all returned by the next ferry to New Jersey by late afternoon. It was a good day out and everybody was happy though a bit tired. Dr. Saurav was to return the next day and exchanged the telephone numbers with both Partho and Kamlesh to keep in touch.

<h1 align="center">-39-</h1>

Indrani retired from her school and was given a grand farewell by her colleagues. After twenty years of a hectic and busy life, she suddenly found herself fully free and unoccupied. For the f rst month or so she enjoyed leisure but then she started to feel a vacuum. Her job for the last twenty years was no more, her both the children had grown up and had left home and only husband and wife remained in the f at, Santanu was also contemplating to leave the job as he was not feeling happy there. She felt the empty nest syndrome, so common when the children leave home, about which she had heard from others, but now was experiencing f rst hand. Her main problem was to keep herself occupied.

Bipasha and Anshuman came back from a very memorable honeymoon trip including a visit to Bist family's ancestral home in Chamba and then started their life together in Anshuman's f at at Model Town. Bipasha remained very busy in setting up the household for about a week and in getting used to a fully independent new married life together. She was not good at cooking but Anshuman was a better cook and helped her in her initial days. By next week she started going to the Lab and soon fell into the groove of her research work as well as balancing her married life with the career.

The next Bhagidari meeting with the Govt. of Delhi was arranged in Azad Bhawan in I.T.O. and Himadri RWA was also invited. Agrawal prepared a letter for Delhi Jal Board, complaining about the falling water pressure in the pipelines consequent to which the overhead tanks on the roof remained partially f lled only and the residents of the RWA always faced scarcity of water. The Chief Engineer replied that with the increasing population of the area there is bound to be increasing water scarcity in future unless the existing main pipeline was changed with larger dia pipes. He also complained that many residents were using online booster pumps thus sucking more quantum of water for their use and that was an added cause of scarcity. His boss immediately instructed him to inspect and catch the culprits with the imposition of heavy penalty as use of online boosters was illegal. The concerned Joint Secretary instructed the Chief Engineer to immediately prepare a cost estimate for changing the main pipeline and get the budgetary approval from him. The chief minister's P.A. gave them a time frame of three months and asked them to send a compliance report to him.

Indranil was by now a chartered accountant and working in a f rm at Nehru Place. He pressed his mother to go to Nilanjana in US Chittaranjan Park had some very good quality homemade Bengali food tiff n career services available and after arranging one on monthly basis for her son, Lopamudra decided to go to Nilanjana in New Jersey by last week of April.

Sushovan and Nilanjana received Lopamudra at the JFK airport in New York. Nilanjana's belly had just started to show up, her face was radiating the complacent glow of an expecting mother and she was very happy to see her mother in USA. In the evening Suman came to visit her and told "my in-laws are also coming to stay with us for a few months. It would be good, aunty, that you would also be here, they would get your company".

In June Jay Shankar and Jaya also came to visit their son for the f rst time in US. Their grandson Abhishek was now almost four years old. Saurav telephoned his mother that he was stuck up with his hospital duties and would visit them in September.

Kamlesh had cleared her second-semester courses also very well. Mrinalini had already submitted her thesis and was due to leave by end of the month and Sunita was to leave by next month by which time they had to vacate the house. Fortunately, the accommodation problem of Kamlesh was sorted out very amicably. Amanda invited her to stay with them, she had an extra room and since she as well as Pamela knew her well, the arrangement worked out well. By the end of July Kamlesh shifted to Amanda's house. Amanda conf ded "once in a while, in connection with audit work, my company expects me to stay overnight and f nish the outstation work. I have been refusing it until now thinking about Palmela but now with you here, I can leave her safely in trusted hands and accept those assignments."

During summer holidays, Kamlesh was concentrating on her research work. Her supervisor Dr. Bloomenthal who was an associate professor in the department was very happy with her progress and asked her to submit a progress report of her research work. She submitted her report by August f rst week and when her supervisor went on a three-week vacation, she also went for a few days to New Jersey.

Nilanjana's son was born in a hospital in June and was now more than a month old, her whole time was now devoted to the tending of her son. Lopamudra had taken complete charge of managing the household, leaving her daughter to devote her full time to the newborn baby. In the evening Suman and Mrs. Jay Shankar came and Suman introduced Kamlesh to her mother-in-law while Abhishek ran and clung to Kamlesh. "She is doing her Ph.D. in the University of Syracuse."

Jaya said, "Abhishek seems to know her well".

Nilanjana replied "she is the best friend of my friend in Delhi and has come to our house several times. She knows Dr. Saurav also."

Jaya said "unfortunately he is stuck up with his hospital duties and is unable to come this month."

The new semester started and Kamlesh again got busy with her studies. She was now living with Amanda and Pamela was very happy to have her company.

Simon came back to New York after a self-imposed exile in Paris for a year. Manish went to the airport to receive him and coaxed him to stay with him in Manhattan. Simon surrendered his rented accommodation, moved in at 106th street, and got a job in a printing f rm. Manish had completed more than f ve years with being HIV positive, was maintaining good health and was leading a good life. Simon sold his share of the restaurant business to his brother Henk and with the money, they purchased the f oor of the house where they were living. People in due time came to know the relationship of Manish and Simon but by now such relationships had become quite open in New York, thanks mainly due to 'gay liberation' rallies and movement. Now lesbians and gays were pressing for same-sex marriages to be made legal but there was opposition from the Church. However, it was considered to be only a matter of time before such marriages were legalized. New Yorkers, in general, did not much bother about the morality or immorality of a relationship and they were quite used to having a wide spectrum of odd people living on the brinks around them like hippies, dropouts, militants, gays, lesbians, trans genders, muggers, zombies, crooks and so on.

Strangely enough, Simon's brushes with police also had markedly declined since he had moved out of his Brooklyn neighbourhood. May be the hostility of police, in part, was due to his being a part of that locality. Anyway, since both Simon and Manish were approaching the middle age, they both were quite relieved by the acceptance of Simon in the new neighbourhood. They both continued their annual travels to different parts of the world together, making a few days stopover on their way, to their apartment in Paris also. In time they travelled through Russia, China including Tibet, Polynesia, Newzealand, South America, Central Africa and many remote corners of the world.

Partho had completed two years in Atlanta. His company had rented a house for them in which three of his other colleagues were also staying. His one colleague Haf z Ahmed from Aligarh was a good cook and courtesy to him they often could eat good Mughlai dishes. His other two housemates Reddy from Hyderabad and Srinath from Bangalore were completing their terms and were due to return in a few months. Partho in between had gone twice to New Jersey to meet Sushovan and Nilanjana and had seen, during his last visit, their son in a crawling stage.

Jai Shankar after a few month's stays with his son started feeling restless and homesick in the new environment. He felt people in USA were too busy with their own lives and pursuits and had no time for anything else. He was talking with his son Gautam and asked "how do you like this kind of mechanical sort of life? It seems that people here have no leisure and in spite of all the prosperity, there is too much competition and rat race going on everywhere. Do you feel comfortable in the system? Gautam replied "I have spent more than six years in USA. and by now have got used to this system."

His mother asked," when do you propose to get back to India?"

This was a tough question and Gautam could not give a straight answer, he said: "I want to gather some more experience and the salary structure in India is too low for maintaining a decent lifestyle." He had not told his parents that he had applied for US citizenship which was being processed and was likely to be granted soon.

Jay Shankar asked, "Do you mean to say that you want to stay here permanently?". "I have not yet made up my mind" his son replied.

"But if you delay your going back any further, your salary gap will only go on increasing."

Gautam replied "this country has given me all the opportunities to further my career and I am also well settled here. At present, I don't see how I would be benef tted by going back."

Jay Shankar said, "but if all the brilliant, well qualif ed young people from our country decide to settle down in the greener pastures of West, then the best of Indian education system would seem mainly catering to the needs of the Developed World in providing them with the best-trained professionals."

Gautam countered "that is one angle of looking at the situation but it also means that Indian educational system is getting worldwide recognition and Indian professionals are competing with the best of the world."

Jay Shankar said "well! it also means brain drain from the developing countries."

Gautam said" whatever, but the fact remains that the world has opened up, the globalization process is well underway and in the era of free competition, the national frontiers are fading away. Anyway, these points remain debatable but the fact also remains that in basic sciences if you want to do quality research, you also need well-equipped labs, modern library facilities backed up by proper funding and this is apart from your knowledge. Let us face it that the Indian Labs are miles behind from what we get even in the average Labs here. That is the primary reason why I believe I would not become a better scientist by simply going back there."

His father had to agree" Well! what you say may be quite true but that also implies that basic research is becoming so high tech and expensive that it is progressively becoming out of reach of the developing countries."

Dr. Gautam nodded" It may be unfortunate but the sad truth remains, at least for any world-class research. Jaya, who was listening all the while, now chipped in "if Saurav also starts thinking on the same lines, my both the brilliant sons will end up becoming N.R.I.s.

Suman said, "let devarji f rst f nish his FRCS, but even if he decides to settle here, all of us would be very happy if you could come and stay with us permanently."

Jaya continued "Saurav is not yet married, let us hope that at least he does not end up in marrying an American girl. In that case, I, at least, would not feel comfortable in his home."

Suman looked at her husband and hesitatingly said:" I have observed that devarji is developing some interest in an Indian girl…"

Jaya immediately became inquisitive "has he told you anything?"

"Not yet, but he is a great admirer of her".

"Who? have you seen her? Do we know her?" She looked at Suman. Suman again looked at her husband and replied "yes, you also have seen her, she is Kamlesh."

"You mean the one who was in Nilanjana's house?"

"Yes, yes, the same one" assured Suman. Jaya said, "but she is very young, should be 8 to 9 years younger to him". Dr. Gautam admonished his wife "you have already started harbouring romantic dreams about them too soon, they have to think about it f rst."

Jaya countered "why? What is wrong with Saurav. He is a very eligible bachelor, any girl would be fortunate to have him as a husband."

Jay Shankar reminded his wife "that's what we had thought about Shreya also" Jaya became silent with the bitter memory and a heavy silence descended on the scene for a while. Gautam came out of it f rst "but Kamlesh has gone through a major tragedy so recently, she may not even be inclined to think about it so soon."

Both his parents looked up "what about the tragedy?"

He looked at Suman "you tell them" and she narrated the story.

Jaya was shocked "what a scoundrel that boy was! I can see how much that poor girl must have suffered. May God bless her!!"

Suman told rest of the story "her parents wanted her to come back but she decided to carve out her destiny in this country only, self-supported her by doing odd jobs, passed the required entrance tests and now is pursuing graduate studies for a Ph.D. after winning a scholarship."

Jay Shankar was very impressed" that girl sure has a nerve of steel, only a Punjabi girl will have such a nerve. Our girls would have wilted long back."

Suman became bolder and asked "Ma, if you approve the match, I could proceed further. "Jaya gave her consent "My wholehearted approval for her. She is very pretty also and has not hidden her past like that Lucknow girl. You may go ahead". Jay Shankar advised some caution "my feeling is to let Saurav decide and take the initiative. Let there be no more face losing for us this time" and everybody agreed.

Jai Shankar asked his son to arrange for their return tickets next month. Gautam asked, "Dad, what is the hurry?" Jai Shankar replied "we have already been here over three months. Frankly speaking, we are old people and are unable to adjust to the lifestyle here. I am missing my friends and the familiar environment."

Gautam said, "you stay for some more time and slowly you will f nd it acceptable". "No, son! you are young and your whole life lies ahead whereas I have crossed working age and am in the last phase of my life. I am happier by being there because I have a sense of belonging to that place. Here we feel like strangers. We will come to visit you again but as far as I am concerned Kanpur is our place", he looked at his wife who nodded. Gautam was not satisf ed "it may be your place now as you both are physically f t it but I am thinking of say ten years hence. Don't you think it would be better if you stayed here?" Jay Shankar said, "in fact, I have a third option."

"What?"

"you know, my youngest brother, Mani Shankar who was in the Indian army and was badly injured in Kashmir while f ghting terrorists?

"Yes, who took voluntary retirement from the army after being in hospital for more than a year and whose son Sunil was very dull in studies, and could not pass high school and left studies altogether."

"Yes, the same one. He went back to our ancestral village Khatauli and is now doing agriculture on our land, Sunil is also helping him and it seems both are doing well. Sunil has turned out to be a good farmer, is now married and has a son and a daughter, the son, may be two years older than Abhishek."

Suman asked, "but you were talking of a third option?"

Jay Shankar replied "yes, I am coming to that. See, we keep going to them once in a while and they seem very well adapted to the rural setup and contended with the simple life there. For the last two visits, Mani is asking us to come and live with them and asking me to start my practice there as there is no good doctor in the vicinity" he looked at his wife.

Gautam said, "but after having lived in big cities for such a long time, would you like the life in a village?"

Jaya said "In fact, Kanpur has become too crowded and cramped and as we are getting old, we feel that we don't need all the trapping of the busy city life but rather a calm and quiet life. Khatauli has electricity and is connected by a good road to Meerut. We can have all the amenities of modern life there also, have a car for mobility and your father can start practice, primarily to keep himself busy."

Jay Shankar added "we have enough space there and can build a small house for ourselves also with plenty cash still remaining if we dispose our f at in Kanpur and move over to Khatauli. We have not taken any decision yet but that option is still open.

Nilanjana's son was also more than four month's old so Lopamudra also felt like going. In the last week of November Jay Shankar, Jaya and Lopamudra boarded the f ight from New York to Delhi together and returned.

-40-

Shweta and Sudhakar were now in the f nal year of their M.B.A., their romance had now become public and a hot topic of speculation. They were going steady and had dreams of marriage in their eyes. Sudhakar had taken Shweta to his parents and had made his intentions clear to them. Bansals were nice people, Mrs. Bansal was a lecturer in Kamla Nehru College, near Asiad village. Their daughter was already married and Bansals were relieved that their son had made up his mind. Shweta had likewise taken Sudhakar to her home and had announced her intentions to marry him and Kauls were happy about it. Toward the end of their f nal year classes, campus interviews were held by big companies with job offers and both Shweta and Sudhakar were selected for advance placements–Shweta by a multinational company in Chennai and Sudhakar by an Indian I.T. Company in Bangalore. After the f nal exams were over Kaul and Sukriti went to Bansals to talk about the marriage and then f x a date some times in May, so that the newlywed couple could live together also for a while till their results were out and they join their assignments in Chennai and Bangalore.

Kauls had booked the Sadiq Nagar community centre for the marriage. Agrawal made his f at available to Kaul and as most of his relatives were local, this solved the accommodation problem for the marriage. The marriage went off well and Kaul sponsored the honeymoon trip of the couple to Kulu-Manali after which Shweta went away to live with the Bansals. By the middle of June, the MBA results were out, both had cleared it with good marks and by the f rst week of July both of them had to join their assignments in different cities. Kaul went along with his daughter to Chennai where he had booked his bank's guest house for a week, to settle her down in her new environment. Shweta joined the M.N.C. while Sudhakar joined the I.T.

company in Banglore. Shweta's colleagues had arranged a company leased furnished f at in a posh locality for her and after settling Shweta in the new address, Kaul returned to Delhi.

After joining their posts, for a few months, Sudhakar and Shweta kept visiting each other on alternate weekends to be together every week. Sudhakar was Asst. Manager in an Indian I.T. Company but his pay package was less attractive than Shweta even through her designation was lower than him. Both were realizing that they should live together and living separately was the hurdle between them and happy married life, apart from the f nancial saving incurred in keeping a single establishment. However, there was a small impasse. Shweta did not want to leave her job at Chennai because any job at Bangalore was not able to match her present salary and she did not want to join at a lower salary. Instead, she insisted Sudhakar come over to Chennai but there his hitch was that he did not want to go on a lower designation. They kept applying for jobs at both ends but were unable to get a satisfactory placement. Shweta called her parents to visit her. Sukriti had retired from her school a few months back and Kauls decided to visit their daughter in January.

Sukriti was shocked to see her daughter's lifestyle in Chennai. She had no arrangement for cooking in her posh apartment. On her asking, Shweta replied" I go early in the off ce, have my breakfast, lunch and evening tea in the company canteen as we are provided subsidized coupons for the purpose by the company. At night also I order the dinner on home delivery service on a monthly arrangement. So there is no necessity for having any cooking arrangement."

Sukriti was not satisf ed" how can you eat South Indian food on a regular basis?"

"Ma, initially it was diff cult but by now I am accustomed. Moreover, it saves the botheration to buy grocery, vegetables etc. apart from cooking and washing the utensils."

"But when Sudhakar comes on the weekends, don't you feel like having some home-cooked food?"

Shweta confessed, "Initially I had tried but soon enough I found out that I am a lousy cook, besides I don't also enjoy cooking."

Sukriti exchanged a glance with her husband and said "whatever, but we would like to have homemade food as long as we are here and you better make all the arrangements fast."

"O.K., I will come early from the off ce in the evening and then we would go to the 'Spencers' and buy whatever is necessary. For lunch today I will order north Indian food for you by home delivery."

After she went to the off ce by an off ce car, Sukriti told her husband in a very disappointing tone. "She does not behave like a married Indian woman. She is living like in a transit camp and has no inclination to make this place her home as if staying in a hostel. A home without cooking is unthinkable for me". Kaul said" She is a working woman and is in a high-pressure job. May be she does not have time for these daily chores." Sukriti fumed "I was also a working woman and in addition, I had two young children also but I had been managing my home front quite successfully all these years". Kaul said "But we did not have this kind of money in those days at our young age. We could not even dream to be able to afford to lead this kind of a lifestyle at such a young age." Sukriti was not convinced "no doubt, she is doing very well for her age, but the job only can not give you all that you want in life. I don't know why the young people are running after money like mad these days and missing all other funs in the bargain. She is a married woman but living like a bachelor. I doubt whether Sudhakar will feel this place his home even though his wife lives here. Besides, I have a strong belief that unless husband and wife stay together, they will not develop the necessary understanding to accept each other with all their shortcomings and faults."

Shweta came back early in the evening and they went to 'Spencers', big departmental stores. Sukriti bought the utensils, groceries, vegetables and other tidbits and they came home. Sukriti started the kitchen, which fortunately had a gas cylinder, cooked food and Shweta also ate it with relish. While clearing the dining table Sukriti asked: "by the way, at what time does your maid come?"

'Ma, actually there is no maid as my comings and goings do not have any regular hours. They all insist for a f xed timing and are not f exible at all. Moreover, there is also a very serious language problem. So I decided to do away with them." Shweta hesitatingly said.

"But then who cleans the house?". "I do it, on the weekends." Said Shweta.

Sukriti was not satisf ed, "that is why the whole place looks so unkempt." Then she looked at her and said:"anyway since now I am here, you better arrange for one right away." Shweta went to the next-door neighbour whose maid used to work earlier with her also and arranged to get her back in the morning.

Next day after coming from the off ce Shweta found the house very spic and span and things arranged nicely. She hugged her mother "Oh! ma, you stay with me permanently."

Sukriti was pleased and said. "we would love to, but we have our own house in Delhi also."

"Oh! you sell that house and move in with me here "she looked at her father.

While having tea, Sukriti told her" see, it is the wife's duty to convert a house into a home and mind you, it is not done with money, much more important is your care, personal involvement and attention."

"But ma! I have to work."

"Even then it remains the responsibility of the woman."

Shweta protested "It is very unfair to the woman, why is God so partial to men?"

"No, it is not a question of being partial. See! God has given the responsibility to the woman to bear and rear the children and has accordingly equipped her with necessary hormones and emotions, she is thus instinctively a homemaker. Men are not as prof cient to do the household chores, they have a much better aptitude for managing the external world."

Shweta protested" Ma, you are very partial to men" and then looked at her father "do you also think so?"

"I also feel that women are more suited, both emotionally and mentally, to take care of the home front. It is a matter of division of labour–woman manages home front not only bearing children but rearing them also is an exclusive domain of mother. "Man manages the outside world." Sukriti asked," whose turn is it to visit this week-yours or Sudhakar's?"

"Mine, because last week he had come here." Sukriti told her "Now since we have come, we would like our son-in-law to come to us on every weekend and feel the difference. You better telephone him right away and invite him here on our behalf." Shweta did so and Sudhakar gladly agreed to the proposal.

He reached by Shatabdi Express early on a Saturday morning and was very pleased to see the change in the house, besides eating the homemade north Indian food.

After lunch, the question of their living together resurfaced on the dining table. Sudhakar complained, "Uncle, I have so many times requested Shweta to change her job and come over to Bangalore but she is not even willing to consider it."

Shweta countered "why don't you agree to shift to Chennai?"

Kaul mediated "O.K., let us f rst hear his problem."

Sudhakar explained "See uncle! I work in an Indian I.T. company. Our pay packets are not comparable to MNCs where she is working but even then I am getting a decent salary of ₹60,000 plus. My designation is that of Asst. Manager and within a year or so, based on my performance appraisal which is very good till date, my boss feels that I should be elevated to the level of Manager, with a minimum increase of about ₹8000/- per month, apart from increased perks "he looked at Kaul and then added, "that is why don't want to leave my present job so soon."

Kaul had to admit "it looks quite reasonable to me "and then asked Shweta "Now, what are your reservations?" She said "I agree that his designation is a very plus point for him and if he is elevated to the post of Manager, it would be quite an achievement. Having said so, let me also tell you that my present pay packet is ₹ Seventy thousand plus, with a provision of annual increment of ₹ f ve to ten thousand, based on performance. They also send the best achiever in the department to a six-month training in USA with the promise of a promotion. I am currently among the front rankers for the US training and that is why I also can't leave the job so soon, at least not without trying for the reward."

Sukriti intervened "if you both remain adamant about your positions, the problem would drag on. I Suggest, one of you to compromise."

Shweta quipped "but which one?"

Sukriti said, "if you ask my opinion, I would say it has to be you".

Shweta was not amused "this looks unfair to me but anyway, explain why?" "because men traditionally are supposed to be the primary earners and the main responsibility to provide f nancial security to the family lies with them." Shweta countered "O.K. agreed, but in this case, I am the primary earner." Sukriti shrugged "that does not change the equation."

Shweta was furious "Ma, being a woman, you are accepting this subordinate role?". Sukriti was adamant "exactly, being not only a woman but in addition after also having the experience of raising a family, I am convinced of this."

"Please explain why?"

Sukriti argued "you really want to know why? because it is a matter of time before you get pregnant whereby you will have to leave your job for at least two to three years. Your motherhood would demand it." Shweta interrupted her "but suppose I do not want to have a child now?". Sukriti replied, "See, God has prescribed a ripe age for childbearing as well as rearing the children and mind you that it does not depend on whether you are an M.B.A. or working in a multinational". Sudhakar clapped loudly "I was afraid to drive home this point, scared that she would jump at my throat calling me a male chauvinist pig, thank you, aunty!" Shweta admonished "She is not any more your aunty".

"Sorry, thank you Ma", Sudhakar corrected himself.

Shweta looked at her father for support, who only said "Well! unless you refuse altogether to become a mother, the equation would more or less remain the same. It may be unfair to a woman but nature has its own priorities."

Sudhakar proposed "let us go to see some Hindi movie and everybody agreed. Kauls returned to Delhi after a month but Sukriti extracted a promise from Shweta that she would prepare her own breakfast and dinner and would retain the maid who had agreed to come at seven in the morning and to f nish her work before Shweta left for the off ce.

○○○

-41-

For the last few months, Agrawal had started having a strange feeling in his heart. He was already past seventy-f ve and was still reasonably active but lately, his physical faculties were slowing down. His hearing was getting impaired; it was becoming increasingly diff cult to hear from the left side; he was already having some problem with his vision, he was getting colour blind and he could not stand bright sunlight or intense light. The specialists had opined that his optic nerve was drying up, they had prescribed medicines but the effect was only marginal if any. He had been advised to wear deep coloured sunglasses while going out during day time, avoid direct sunlight and use a walking stick for outdoor work but all these were restricting his free movement. On top of that, his hands trembled while writing, so much so, that his bank signatures were often not tallying creating problems with money transactions. He could realize that his body was wilting, his body was no longer extending him the necessary co-operation to lead an independent life and things were going from bad to worse.

Another aspect, which he had carefully hidden from even his daughters also, was that the expensive cancer treatment of Nandini had heavily drained his resources. His own medical insurance didn't cover his increasing medical expenses and his main worry was in case of any major illness or prolonged hospitalisation, the exorbitant hospital charges of Delhi being what they were, how he was going to meet the expenses. This was apart from the fact that he was living alone and could depend on no one to take his care during medical emergencies. All through his life he had lived independently and did not want to live with his daughters also, becoming dependent on them.

He did not know how many more years he had to live; he prayed to God not to take away the bounty of good health that he had enjoyed all through his life. Lately, however, it seemed that God was not granting him the favour, obviously, everybody must be praying for the same. If he was now given a choice to end his life, he would gladly accept the offer. His daughters were well settled, his wife was gone, he was satisf ed with the good life that he was fortunate to lead up to now. Looking back through the long years that was already behind him, his memory was still very good, he had no regrets. His several close friends and relatives were already gone, he had not much wished to live any further. He wanted to go with dignity before he became crippled or incapacitated with old age.

A strange thought was lately germinating in his inner heart. Yes! he had a choice in his death, he could voluntarily end his life before it was too late and his independent movements were severely restricted. That was it'. He had absolved himself from all social responsibilities and commitments to his near and dear ones, he had made full use of his capabilities and potentials and his going would not cause any problems to anybody. His daughters will be sad and would grieve for some time but then they as well as the other well-wishers would accept it. Having thus crystallized his thought process and coming to a def nite conclusion, sort of rejuvenated him, it recharged him, so to say, to face the life again. His RWA colleagues noticed this change. Kaul asked him "Agrawalji, you seem to look very happy lately, what is the secret?"

"No, no, nothing secret about it; I have decided to live happily and that's it."

Kaul sighed "I wish I also could say so". "why? What is preventing you?" Agrawal looked at him along with the other members also present in the RWA off ce.

Kaul told them the story of Shweta's self-created problems. Agrawal could only say" well! she only can sort out her problems, so why worry?"

Agrawal decided to take steps to implement his action plan. As a f rst step, he decided to consolidate his f nancial holdings. Over a period of one year, he encashed his mutual funds, shares, F.Ds. etc. in various banks and institutions and transferred everything to his Federal Bank account, which was just near the Jahanpanah Park entrance and where he had a joint account with his youngest daughter. He did not stand for next RWA election and Kaul was elected President. He also opened his f at as a meeting place of the retired people of his RWA and others and by the end of a year it became a quite well-known joint for the elderly people, who occasionally used to celebrate their own birthdays, the birth of a grandson or promotion of their sons etc. all sponsored by the concerned families. The f at became a sort of club, the maintenance of which was looked after by the press wallah's second son, who was appointed by the club members, as a caretaker, being paid from the joint contribution of the members.

Agrawal then made a will, in the presence of an Advocate and signed by two witnesses, Dr. Sharma of Gangotri Apt. and Arora of Neelachal and got the will notarized. As per it, his f at was to be rented out on a monthly rent of ` ten, for the next ten years after his death, as a meeting place of the aged people of the area and made his three daughters as the trustees of the f at. After ten years his daughters could jointly sell the f at or decide what was to be done with it. His cash holdings were to be distributed equally between his daughters instructing the Federal Bank accordingly and left a sealed copy of the will with the Bank Manager and another with the President of the RWA. The original will was with the advocate L.K. Kapoor who had his off ce in the G.K.-II, 'M' Block Market.

Agrawal called a meeting in the evening in his f at and announced "the time is perhaps ripe to propose a formal name to this meeting place of the elderly people" and looked around" why don't you suggest some names?" Various names were suggested, a vigorous discussion followed and ultimately a name suggested by Santanu 'Oldies joint' was accepted.

Bhanot was entrusted to get the name of its members entered in a new register whereas Santanu was asked to prepare a proforma of the membership form, get it typed, get it duly f lled up by the members and store it as a document of the organization. Agrawal suggested Subramanium prepare a constitution and then call a meeting to get it approved, followed by an election of the off ce bearers, to give a f nal shape to its formal existence. In the meeting, the constitution was approved and Agrawal was elected its f rst President and Santanu the secretary. Somebody suggested to get the 'Oldies joint' registered also with the Delhi government and the job was entrusted to Secretary to do the needful. The meeting was attended by twenty-seven members and thus the 'Oldies Joint' became formally operational. It was also proposed to charge a monthly subscription of ` twenty each, to meet the day to day expenses of the club, including the salary of the caretaker Chhotu. Treasurer Bhanot's job was to collect the subscription and keep the accounts. The club timings were def ned- 9:00 A.M.-11:00 A.M., mornings and 6:00 P.M. to 9:00 P.M., evening. Within a few months 'Oldies, Joint' became very popular and members from nearby RWAs also jointed it and in six month's time, the membership swelled to ninety and in next six month's time the joint got registered with the Delhi govt.

Agrawal's left ear had become totally deaf and ongoing to Dr. Rajendra Prasad Eye Centre in AIIMS to get his eyesight tested they asked him to get admitted for a couple of days for thorough testing. The results were more discouraging. Over a period of one year, there had been a signif cant acceleration of the progressive deterioration which implied complete blindness was only a matter of time and medicines were not helping. The optic nerve was indeed drying and there was no chance of it getting restored. The doctors felt within two years or so, at this rate, he won't remain capable of free movement without the aid of others.

Agrawal was worried. He felt that his time for bidding goodbye had arrived. Any further delay would mean that he won't remain capable to implement the scheme. With the f nal decision made, he encashed all his. F.Ds and deposited it in his account in Federal Bank. Over a period of time, he went to various chemist's shops and complaining insomnia, bought four tablets of sleeping pills each time, not to arouse any suspicion. Neighbourhood Delhi chemists are very obliging if you don't ask for any receipt, the norm being, no receipt, no questions. He thus collected forty tablets in about a month, withdrew ten thousand rupees from the bank and went by train on a short trip, to Nainital in the f rst week of December leaving the keys of his f at with the secretary of the Oldies Joint.

From Kathgodam he took a taxi to Nainital and checked in a posh hotel in Mallital, near the zoo. For two days he went around the tourist spots, the boat ride in the lake, tiger and panther caves, suicide point, other lakes around the city limits, China peak etc. He bought a fancy looking walking stick from the upper Mall road and on the third day after breakfast walked up to the suicide point, surveyed the spot around it and familiarized himself with the way by again walking there in the afternoon.

After returning to his hotel he wrote farewell letters to all his three daughters, one letter to Dr. Sharma in Gangotri Apartment to read out a copy of the will to the Secretary 'Oldies Joint', one letter to Advocate Kapoor to inform about his death to his elder daughter and summon all the three daughters to Delhi to read out his Will. The last letter was addressed to the Hotel Manager, Joshi:

Many thanks for the wonderful hospitality during my stay here. I have cleared all my bills and have checked out of your hotel. By the time you receive this letter, I will not be alive. I am leaving this world of my own free will and being fully satisf ed with my life. Please inform about my demise to :

Sri L.K. Kapoor, Advocate

'M' 2/4, Greater Kailash-II, New Delhi-110019.

I am enclosing ₹2000/- in cash in the envelope to please arrange the funeral in case the body is found. Good Bye.

L.N. Agrawal

Room No. 14

He put all the letters in separate envelopes, put the envelope of Mr.Joshi in a separate sealed cover and next morning after early lunch cleared his bills and checked out of the hotel. He put his bills in the coat pocket and deposited the suitcase in the counter saying that he would come back after some time, and then collect his luggage.

From the hotel he went to the Post Off ce by a hotel taxi, posted all the letters by Registered Post, bought a book and a bottle of water from a nearby shop, asked the taxi to take him to the main road (near the suicide point), cleared the taxi bills with a heavy tip and the taxi went away. He kept walking, turned away from the road and reached the suicide point. It was a sunny afternoon and the tourist season had not yet started. One family had come to see the suicide point, they took some photos and in a while went away.

Agrawal kept sitting for some time on the boulder reading the book and looked below. There was a gorge about six hundred feet deep, mostly rocky and quite steep. The sun was to go behind the opposite hill in about another half an hour and it was getting chilly. The place was deserted and he looked all around, nobody was there. He took out the bottle of the sleeping pills from his coat pocket, gulped the pills in several instalments with the help of water from the bottle till he f nished all the pills. The sun had gone behind the hills, dusk and darkness was rapidly creeping in and he was already feeling drowsy. He took a few steps to the edge and jumped into the deep gorge down below. The effect of the pills had already started, his drowsiness was increasing, so much so that with the fall when he crashed against some branches of the trees, landed with a heavy thud on a rock, rolled another hundred feet or so down and f nally rested against a big boulder, he did not feel any pain and that was the last thing he remembered. Down below where he had landed, it was already quite dark and a deadly silence prevailed all around.

The hotel Manager had been informed by his evening shift staff that the tourist of Room No. 14 had not yet taken away his suitcase but when he received the letter next morning by a post he got alarmed. He called the police and showed them the letter. The police questioned him, called the taxi driver but he had gone with the tourists on some local sightseeing trip. On his return, he told police that the old man with sunglasses and a stick had f rst gone to the Post Off ce, then to a book shop and had f nally left the taxi on the main road saying that he would walk back and he showed them the point. The Police straightway went to the suicide point, found a walking stick which the taxi driver identif ed belonging to the old man. They tried to look down below into the gorge but nothing was visible due to the vegetation.

Next day police sent a search party into the gorge and by afternoon discovered a badly mutilated body from the bottom, which was brought to the police station and identif ed as that of Agrawal by the receipts of the hotel and post off ce and his identity card. As the dead body had already started emanating a smell, the police arranged a small funeral as per the last wishes of the deceased and also informed the Delhi Police who informed advocate Kapoor, who by this time had already received the letter and had informed the three daughters of the deceased.

Dr. Sharma came to the 'Oldies Joint', gave the sad news and read out the Will to the people. A pall of gloom descended on the RWA and the whole neighbourhood.

Agrawal's three daughters had come to their late father's f at. Reema read out her letter f rst:

Nainital

dated..............

Dear Reema,

I have very sweet memories of this place as, more than forty years back, I had come to this place for our honeymoon with my wife. You must have been shocked to know about my demise and as your father, I owe you an explanation. I am already eighty years old and lately, the old age is taking its toll on me.

I have become almost deaf in my left ear, with the right one also deteriorating; my hands tremble badly due to Parkinson's disease consequent to which my bank signatures often do not tally; I can not stand bright sunlight and my eyesight is also progressively weakening because my optic nerves are drying up, for which there is no cure. The doctors inform me that within a year my vision will not remain enough to permit me free unassisted movement. In short, I am becoming seriously physically handicapped.

I have led a clean, independent, active and dignif ed life all through and can not foresee, me leading a crippled, helpless and vegetative existence like your mother during her last days. I have lived my life, played my innings to my full satisfaction and thus have no regrets. I intend to go before I lose my independence.

Twentieth-century has bestowed us the rights to live with dignity but unfortunately, due to hangovers from the old morality laws, it is still unable to provide us with the same degree of dignity in our death also. Hope, the twenty-f rst century into which we have already been ushered, will take this into account and would legalise euthanasia or quick mercy killing under special terminal circumstances. Well! I have chosen a quick end from a terminally handicapped life. Please bear with the eccentricity of your old father. With all the blessings to all of you.

–Your father

She was sobbing all the way while reading the letter. Both her other sisters also conf rmed that they had received similar letters. Next day advocate Kapoor came and read out the will in presence of the witnesses, Federal Bank Manager and President of the RWA. Federal Bank manager distributed the money between the three daughters, the police handed them the death certif cate as well as the suitcase sent by the Nainital Police. With the formalities done, the daughters arranged a Shraddha ceremony, followed by kirtan, then left the f at to the 'Oldies Joint' and left.

-42-

By the end of the fourth semester, Kamlesh had cleared all her course requirements with very good grade point averages. Head of the Department of Biological Sciences asked the graduate students who had f nished their course requirements, to appear for a comprehensive exams due to be held in the month of May, to decide the best ones who would to be allowed to proceed directly for Ph.D. while the rest would have to f rst do the masters and would then be allowed to proceed for Ph.D. After the comprehensive exams, her research guide Dr. Bloomenthal congratulated her and said" the Research Committee has recommended that you could proceed straight for Ph.D. and since your credit requirements are over, it means you will henceforth devote your full time to research work. She discussed her research project and asked her to submit the research proposal in a fortnight, to be approved by the Research Committee." As an afterthought, she also added" and yes, the Research Committee has approved to give you a raise of 100 dollars per month in your scholarship starting this month."Next day the list was put out in the departmental notice board. Two other students besides her were going straight for Ph.D, eight were going for Masters and one had been asked to quit, based on performances.

Kamlesh was very happy after a long time and phoned Nilanjana, who congratulated her and complained "we haven't seen you for a long time. Why don't you take a break for a few days and spend some time with us."

Kamlesh replied "I would love to but before that, I have to submit my research proposal within a fortnight. I would be able to come there by the second week of June, I feel."

Suman was sitting by her side when Nilanjana received the phone and she also congratulated Kamlesh. On reaching home, she phoned Dr. Saurav also and teased him "better come here during the second week of June if you want to see her also."

Next day Dr. Saurav telephoned Kamlesh "Can you recognize the voice of your admirer?"

"Is this Dr. Saurav?

"Oh, you get full marks for correct identif cation but I still have a complaint". "O.K., shoot it right away "she also playfully said.

"I had expected to hear the good news straight from the horse's mouth but it reached me only through Suman bhabhi." She said "Oh that! I f gured it would only be routine news for you."

"Why, why?".

"Because I have learnt from the same source that both of you brothers were very bright students throughout your careers." He cut her short "so, now you can also safely include you in that list" and congratulated her. They talked for some more time and before concluding he asked her "when can I expect to see you in New Jersey?"

"By the second week of June, "she replied. "Well, then it is settled that we will meet there during that time, good night" he kept the receiver.

After submitting her research proposal, Kamlesh took a leave for one week and started for New Jersey. Partho came to the bus station to receive her. Nilanjana's son Shyamal, nicknamed, Mantu had just started walking, had become the cynosure of the whole house and kept everybody on their toes. Nilanjana informed her "my mother left in December, Mantu had become very attached to her and had cried for several days after she left."

After dinner, Partho and Kamlesh were talking in their room. Partho was in USA for more than two years now and he wanted to share a secret with her "Didi, I am presently in a great dilemma but I can't discuss it with anybody in my family. Can you help me out?"

"What is it? "Kamlesh looked at him" that is if you can conf de in me?"

He confessed shyly "I am getting involved, it seems, with a Canadian girl who lives alone in the same apartment building in Atlanta."

"Why are you telling me about this, it is your personal matter."

"I know but still I want your advice."

"O.K., shoot?"

He showed her a photograph "She is from Quebec city and is a French Canadian, living in Atlanta for the last four years and working in the editorial department of a reputed publishing f rm" he looked at her.

"So, what is your problem? "She asked.

"See, we are going out together for the last one year but presently I have reached a stage where I have to decide whether I should continue."

"Why?"

"Because I am getting emotionally involved. If I continue, there may be a point of no return and we have to think in terms of marriage sooner or later."

"So where is the problem?" She asked. "the marriage will also be linked with my decision to stay on in this country permanently and my mother may not like it."

"But do you really want to stay on in this country? If I know correctly, you are on deputation from your company on H1 B visa, which means you have to go back after your term is over" she looked at him. He nodded "exactly "and added but there are ways to come back."

"How?"

"See, one of our clients is offering me a job. At present, I can not take it because I have a bond with my company to serve them for one year after return. If I resign my job after that, the client is prepared to sponsor my H1 B visa and appoint me in their company."

"Well! ultimately it has to be your decision but how is the offer?" She asked.

"I can simply say that the offer is much better".

"So, when are you going back to India?" "in about six months time".

"Well! have you discussed this aspect with your friend and by the way, what is her name?

"Annie,and yes,we have discussed and she is prepared not only to wait but has also assured that she would pursue the case from this end also."

Kamlesh smiled" Annie seems to be a nice girl". He was quick to corroborate "she is the daughter of a professor in Quebec university, has done her masters in economics from Toronto and is a serious girl."

"Well, she def nitely has a good background but if you ask my opinion, I would only say that you should not marry in a haste, your different cultural backgrounds mean you should understand each other well and it is also linked to a large extent with whether you want to live in India or here. In my opinion, it has to be your own choice and don't feel guilty about it. You can call your parents here in their old age or can send them money for emergencies etc. from here also but what is important that you live your life to your full potentials, whether here or there."

"Thank you didi" Partho seemed quite relieved "I needed your advice" and then pressed her hands "why don't you pay a visit to Atlanta, I will arrange your stay there and you will know Annie also." She smiled "in that case, I would like to stay with Annie."

His face immediately brightened "Excellent idea and let us arrange this as soon as possible."

Next morning Dr. Saurav, Partho and Kamlesh went to see a movie. Dr. Saurav was very tied up with his hospital duties, had been able to manage a leave only for the weekend and had come by his car from Boston. Suman had invited Kamlesh, Partho and Sushovans for lunch and by the time Dr. Saurav and his group reached home after the movie, Sushovans were already there. While returning from the movie Kamlesh asked Dr. Saurav "how is your FRCS programme going on?"

"Not bad, it should take me another two years at the max." He asked, "And what about yours?"

"Around the same time, I guess."

Dr. Saurav announced "I have a plan". Partho asked, "you mean after FRCS?" "No, no, for tomorrow".

Kamlesh asked "what?"

"See, I have to go back tomorrow. I say, why don't you both also come along with me and allow me to be your host for a day or two? He looked at Kamlesh. Partho replied "Not a bad idea, we have an off ce in Boston," and he looked at Kamlesh "why don't you come to Atlanta with me for a day or two after that?"

Kamlesh said, "would it not be too hectic?"

Partho countered "so what, we are not yet that old."

Dr. Saurav said "so, that settles it. We leave after lunch tomorrow, I will come to pick you up at say 2 o'clock in the afternoon" and both nodded.

Dr. Saurav picked up Partho and Kamlesh at two o'clock the next day and they started for Boston. Partho drove for the major part and they reached before dark. Dr. Saurav was telling them "Boston is a very historical city for Americans because the war of independence started from here."

Kamlesh asked "independence from whom?" "Well! to start with America was a British colony but gradually the people whose ancestors had originally come from England and had settled here developed their own identity and wanted independence from British sovereignty and started rebellion against the British rule."

Partho commented, "just like India." "yes, and in 1773, some Americans threw 340 boxes of tea into the sea from a few British ships docked in Boston harbour, as a mark of their protest. In retaliation, the British closed the Boston harbour and cancelled the self-rule status of the Massachusetts province. This led to the war of independence and ultimately USA became a free nation on 4th July 1776."

Dr. Saurav was residing in a two-room apartment in the hostel, just outside the premises of Boston Medical School. The hostel was primarily for the interns and junior doctors. He had a night duty so he left after dinner. Next morning, after breakfast Partho left to meet his colleagues in the Boston off ce. Kamlesh was watching T.V. when Dr. Saurav arrived around ten and apologized for the delay "I am sorry to leave you alone but I had a class in the morning." She said, "I was, in fact enjoying the leisure."

"Well, in that case, I will have to leave you again after lunch, I have an O.T. duty again.

"No problem, please feel free". Dr. Saurav said "See, our life is like this only. The hospital sucks you and takes away all your time. You can't work on the basis of scheduled duty hours, in addition, there will be unscheduled irregular hours over which you have no control, on top of these there will be emergency situations. You can't neglect any of them as they are the patients, hospital as well as you, both have an obligation toward them. It is a very hard life."

Kamlesh said "your father was a doctor and I believe nobody forced you to be a doctor?"

"No, no, it was my free decision and after so many years, I have started loving my profession."

"Very nice to hear that though I feel that your profession demands a fair degree of dedication."

"Exactly, but I have arranged for leave tomorrow, after tonight's duty and then we will talk."

Kamlesh said "we were planning to leave for Atlanta by the evening f ight."

"No problem, I will be free for the day tomorrow" and he went to the bathroom took a shower and ordered tea in the room.

While having tea, Kamlesh asked "I am curious to know about the reason for your refusal to marry?"

He looked at her and smiled "I could not tell everything that transpired, to my parents that but I will tell you the reason." and he told her the whole story.

Kamlesh was very impressed "I can now understand that you had a strong reason"

He opined "how can you marry someone even after knowing, that she loves somebody else, it will not be fair to her. I accept that may be the girl had used me to a certain extent but the young man was very keen to marry her and seemed quite committed, so I felt who am I to prevent them from being happy together and so I went along with them and he smiled "let me share a secret with you." I had invited them to spend their honeymoon in my hostel suite in Kanpur and I tell you they both are very good singers", he told her not to tell this to his family members.

She was very touched by his lack of any malice toward them, such chivalry was totally not in tune with the present times.

He continued "the very purpose of marriage is to spend the life happily with each other. Caste, religion and all man-made barriers can not stand any guarantee for happiness."

Kamlesh suddenly remembered her own miserable marriage, tears f lled her eyes, she was choked with emotion and said "alas! if everybody could think like you! I believe you had done the right thing" she looked at him.

Dr. Saurav pressed her hand "do you really think so?"

"Yes, I do" and they kept looking at each other for what seemed to be an eternity, till she lowered her eyes, unable to meet his gaze.

He broke the silence f rst "looking back I now feel that whatever happened was for my own good." "Why?"

"Because otherwise I would not have come to USA and met you "he smiled. She blushed and slowly released her hands from him. Her young woman's heart, no matter how badly bruised, could not remain indifferent to his appeal, and guardedly she said: "I hope you know that I am a married but deserted woman and my present status is only that of an ex-mistress of some crook."

He countered "that is, however, not the only identity you have, to me you are like a phoenix". "and what is that?" she asked.

He explained "Phoenix is a mythical Arabian bird worshipped by ancient Egyptians, which burnt itself to rise once again, rejuvenated from its own ashes" you have come out shining through your Agnipariksha like gold purif ed by f re.

"Whatever but it may not make much difference to change the opinion of your family members."

He held her hands "just forget the past, let us think of a future together". She only said, "give me some time to think".

"Don't take too much time to think. I am already past thirty two, have already missed the bus once, this time I do not want the opportunity to slip through my hands, "he smiled.

Kamlesh as if woke up from a dream, she stood up and said 'be patient."

"But why?" he insisted.

"Because I had made a promise to myself in my darkest hours."

"and what was that?"

"That from here on I will take charge of my own destiny and my f rst goal would be to complete my studies i.e. Ph.D. and then only I would decide my next goal."

He was still hopeful "I will wait, in fact by that time I should also complete my FRCS." He stood up with a tone of f nality "so it is then settled."

She was surprised "what is settled?". "why we just made a deal.?" "What deal?" She protested.

"That we would get married after you complete your Ph.D."

She protested "but I have not yet given my consent."

"But I am giving my consent to you and I am sure that you will also make up your mind before that time."

She said smiling "anyway, let us see."

Dr. Saurav was not yet f nished "O.K., having settled the time limit, could I take you as my f ancée starting today, right?" She was amused "wait! wait!! not so fast. Let us put it this way, we will continue to remain good friends say for a year and then would review the status to see whether to upgrade it further."

He shrugged "whatever, and that would include my coming to Syracuse from time to time to remind you of your commitment made to me."

She thought for a while "O.K. permission granted". Dr. Saurav shook hands with her "thank you, the Boston trip with you was really helpful. We have made so much progress or would we term it as a breakthrough?"

She smiled "you seem to be quite focussed about your goals?"

"I have always been." He disengaged his hands and f nally said "I am hungry, let us go for a quick lunch "and he looked at his watch. They went to the Doctor's café nearby, after lunch, he dropped her in the hostel and went for O.T. duty.

Back in the room, Kamlesh was lost in her thoughts. How fast things had changed in the last few hours. Looking back, she felt that after all, coming to USA though had been very painful to start with, but it had opened the gates for a better future also.

She had to suddenly wake up from her reverie when Partho came back and rang the bell. He talked about his off ce and returned her the credit card which she had given him to buy her ticket. By six in the evening, Dr. Saurav also came back and they went out for dinner. They spent the next day very leisurely and Dr. Saurav dropped them at the airport for their Atlanta f ight in the afternoon. Kamlesh stayed with Annie for two days and found her very amiable, she was prepared to wait for Partho till he came back from India. Partho was very happy to get her approval and introduced Kamlesh with his other housemates. Annie drove her around the city, showed her the town and dropped her at the airport the next day.

The trip to Boston seemed to have a therapeutic effect on Kamlesh. She had hitherto forcibly closed the doors of her heart to any romantic possibilities but somehow she found, Dr. Saurav had managed to sneak through and this changed her perception for the external world. A subtle change in her behaviour pattern was occurring, she seemed happy and started taking interest in people around her. Her change was noticed by Amanda, who observed: "you look very cheerful after your trip to New Jersey and I am really happy about it." Amanda lately often was getting late in returning from the off ce. She shared the secret with her "you know I am dating somebody lately."

Kamlesh came closer to her "really, that is very good to know. How do you f nd him?"

"He is O.K. but I really don't know. We have just started. He is a doctor, you remember, last year when Pamela was hospitalized, he had treated her and she had become very chummy with her. A few months later he had invited us for a hospital social evening and after that we became friends."

Kamlesh said "good that Pamela knows him."

Dr. Saurav used to phone Kamlesh from time to time and during Christmas holidays he paid a visit to Syracuse, checked in a hotel and picked up Kamlesh from the university. They were having tea in the hotel when she informed him "my research proposal has been approved and my research also is progressing satisfactorily."

He said "I have also good news. I have cleared the part two also, now only the f nal remains" and she offered her congratulations.

He asked her "why did you opt for a Ph.D. here, I mean you could have gone for M.B.A. or some I.T. course or could have returned home etc.?"

She replied "the idea was given to me by my best friend, back home. One good thing I had done during my worst days was to have written a letter to her and she had advised me to complete my studies. We were both studying for our M.Sc. at that time in Delhi. She is now almost completing her Ph.D. and has got married also.

He brightened "So, you are following her footsteps."

Kamlesh could not go to New Jersey as she was very busy with her work. Nilanjana informed that her brother Indranil's marriage had been f xed in May and so they would be visiting India during that time. She also informed that Partho had gone back to India last month and had joined in his Bangalore off ce.

-43-

Sushovan and Nilanjana reached Delhi in May for Indranil's marriage. Montoo had by now started talking also but had completely forgotten Lopamudra. Soon he became a darling of the whole house but felt very uncomfortable in the scorching heat of Delhi. The marriage went off very well. The girl Ipsita was an M.B.A. from Jamshedpur, her father working in Tata steel. She was already working in Delhi before marriage at Bhikhaji Cama Place and continued working there after marriage also. During his stay in Delhi, Sushovan visited Jawahar Lal Nehru University (JNU) and Delhi University Biochemistry Deptts and learnt that JNU had advertised the post of Asst. Professor last fortnight. He applied for the post, met the Head of the Department and apprised him his desire of returning to India.

Rajagiri school had opened an evening section 'Vidyashram' where the students of the weaker section of the society of the school were given free tuition to bridge their gap of comprehension with other students. Here the teachers were expected to have one to one contact with the students and remove their def ciencies in specif c areas and subjects. The idea had proved a boon for the economically weaker section society's students and Indrani had volunteered her free services to Vidyashram in order to keep her engaged in the evenings. Bipasha had started writing her Ph.D. thesis and was hoping to submit it before the year-end. The free movements of Mrs.Baluja were quite restricted and she seldom came out of her old age home. Her daughter Garima used to pay her a visit every weekend and collected the rent from the tenant on her behalf. Partho had come to Delhi during Indranil's marriage and was waiting for his one year bond with his company to be ever.

Santanu had left his job in Nehru Place and was now the President of the 'Oldies Joint' which was running smoothly in the late Agrawal's f at. He had seen an advertisement in the paper that the Department of Social Welfare, Government of Delhi, were launching a scheme whereby the registered RWAs or other Senior Citizen groups were to be given government grant to run their institutions subject to fulf lling certain conditions. He discussed the matter with his Managing Committee and took a decision to apply for the grant.

Mrs. Pasricha was by now almost totally bedridden with Arthritis. Anupam had shown her to many eminent doctors but allopathy or physiotherapy could not offer any cure. Anupam and his wife Neha took good care of her. Manish was sending money to keep a nurse permanently for the day time. Mrs. Parashar's only complaint was that Manish was not marrying.

Harish was by now managing his father's business almost independently. Arora was happy that the business was expanding and his son had become capable of handling the business. They were now looking for a match for their son. Kaul and Arora were talking and Kaul asked "Aroraji, did you f nd a girl for Harish?" Arora replied "the search has been made easy by Harish himself. It seems when he was banished to our ancestral village, he met a girl from the village. Both had liked each other and the girl was studying in B.A. at that time. We are going next month to our village to see the girl and talk to her parents."

Kaul had also left the job. Both he and Santanu were keeping them occupied with the RWA, Co-Op Stores, Oldies joint and other such activities and were talking. Santanu said "See, how much our spheres of activities are shrinking. I f nd that unless very much required, we seldom go out of G.K.-II, Alkapuri, Chittaranjan Park belt. Kaul agreed "same with us but we are getting old also and so do not need the hectic pace of our earlier days" he paused and asked, "how is your son?"

Santanu seemed a bit resigned "he is thinking to resign his job in a few months, take up some job in USA and go back to States."

"What about his marriage?"

"He says, after he settles down in his new job there, he will think about his marriage. Indrani did not like the idea and had said let him get married and let his wife be with us, till he was settled in his new job but he didn't agree."

Kaul shrugged "Our children have their own minds and do not think any more like us."

In the month of October, Sushovan alone came on a short visit to Delhi to attend the interview of JNU. By December Partho resigned from his job and went back to USA with another job offer who arranged for his H1 B visa also. By the end of December Bipasha submitted her thesis and came to Indrani for rest of a few days. Sushovan got the job offer from JNU and decided to join the position by the beginning of the next academic session. They decided to return by the end of June from USA.

The 'Oldies joint' received the govt. grant consisting of a one time grant to furnish the house and then the recurring monthly grant to run the organization. The government wanted it to be named as "Recreation Centre" and so the 'Oldies joint' in its new avatar became 'Recreation Centre' with Santanu as its f rst President. The members remembered the farsightedness and kindness of late Agrawalji and paid their homage to him.

EPILOGUE

Dr. Kamlesh Tripathi Asst. Professor at Boston University and Dr. Saurav Tripathi Associate Professor in the Neurosurgery Department in the Harvard Medical school were now US citizens and had a f ve-year-old son Abhimanyu who had just started school. Dr. Gautam Tripathi had moved over to Houston where he was Associate Professor in the Rice University. Dr. Jay Shankar and Jaya Tripathi had ultimately decided to spend rest of their lives in their native village at Khatauli where they had built of a small house for themselves on their land and Jai Shankar had started his private practice with free consultations while Jaya gave honorary service to teach English in the village school.

Partho Chakravarty and Annie were also US Citizens and were now in Los Angeles, California with their six-year-old son Anirban. Santanu and Indrani had visited them several times but had decided to live in Delhi. Bipasha was a lecturer in Gargi College while Anshuman was a reader in Delhi University and they had a daughter Ananya.

Sudhakar and Shweta were now in Bangalore and Bansals had moved over permanently to stay with them. Shweta was now working with an MNC in Bangalore while her daughter had started her schooling. Lately, both Sukriti and Kaul were not keeping good health and were f nding it increasingly diff cult to live independently. they had decided to shift to the Old Age Home in G.K. II where they had already enlisted, were waiting for their turn to come and looking for a buyer for their f at. The 'Recreation Centre' for the senior citizens was quite well-known in their area, with their reading room, library and indoor games facilities, periodic outdoor activities and get-togethers. The local M.L.A. had promised to give them some bigger space in the community centre being built in the area with government funds.

The Bhagidari participation of the RWA was also continuing and in 2009, Himadri RWA had been awarded the best prize among the Delhi RWAs by the Bhagidari authorities and the Chief Minister of Delhi had paid a visit to the RWA. Alas! Agrawal was not there to see the fruits of his labour but people still remembered him. Mrs. Baluja had peacefully died during her sleep in her Old Age Home last year and her daughters had sold her f at.

The gay marriage had been legalized in New York State in 2011 and it was a great victory for the gay liberation front. Simon and Manish had now married off cially and were living as a couple, as had been done by many other gay and lesbian pairs. Mureed and Shreya were now based in Mumbai, had established themselves as professional singers, getting regular calls from Bollywood f lm industry.